LEADING THE
REBELLION

Questing to Succeed in Work and Life

LEADING THE REBELLION

Questing to Succeed in Work and Life

JASON KINGSLEY

First published 2023 by Rebellion
an imprint of Rebellion Publishing Ltd,
Riverside House, Osney Mead,
Oxford, OX2 0ES, UK

www.rebellionpublishing.com

ISBN: 978-1-78108-918-7

10 9 8 7 6 5 4 3 2 1

A CIP catalogue record for this book is available from the
British Library.

Designed & typeset by Rebellion Publishing

Printed in the US

To Paddy, Lulu and Toph.

To Kas and Bok.

Also to the *Silver Brumby* books, Mr. Snuff, Smokey Joe, Twilight
and all the ponies in the distant past that started me on my journey.

Contents

Introduction

I TRY TO live my life according to the Chivalric Code, or rather *a* chivalric code.

There's a lot of misunderstanding about what a chivalric code is. Say 'chivalry' to people, and many of them think you mean a certain form of behaviour by men towards women – opening doors, giving up seats on public transport, even laying your coat across a puddle Walter Raleigh-style. Depending on your point of view, this kind of behaviour is either considerate, polite and gallant or outmoded, unwanted and patronising. Possibly all of those things combined. It is, of course, only a very small part of some of the Chivalric Code.

Chivalry in its original form seems to have developed in the area of what is now France called the langue d'Oc, originally a separate part of that land, with its own language, Occitan, and its own version of Christianity called the Cathar religion, which was brutally supressed by an horrific crusade in those very middle ages. The phenomenon of the troubadour, and of unrequited courtly love which sits alongside the stories of chivalric deeds seems to have been developed there. In brief it was a set of behaviours formulated by society across western Europe and in both Britain and France alike at the time in an effort to control the more base impulses of the warrior class: the knights in the Middle Ages. The etymology of the word itself shows this: 'chivalry' comes from 'chevalerie', the old French word for horsemen. Not just anyone who could ride a horse, but usually a man of aristocratic standing and/or noble ancestry who could equip himself with a war horse and the arms of a heavy cavalryman, and who had been through a variety of rituals too – those rituals being the oaths and initiation ceremonies which involved pledging aspects of the code. Cavalier shares a similar etymology, as does Ritter, the Germanic language equivalent of a noble horse-borne warrior. Interestingly the word 'knight' in English does not come from the same root concept, the horse warrior or roman equites, but from the older Anglo-Saxon word that is variously translated as 'servant' or 'boy', or to make it a bit more modern, 'lads' as in 'one of the lads'.

Over time, however, the meaning of chivalry began to shift, not least because of the growing popularity of the romance genre and its tales of knights errant on heroic and fantastical quests – an early example of the way in which storytelling not just reflects social changes but helps spark those changes too. These stories meant that it was not enough for a knight to be simply brave and skilful in battle: he, and they were invariably he, also had to have moral authority and personal integrity, or at least strive for these attributes even if not reaching perfection. He needed both to possess and to demonstrate what today we would call 'soft' social skills – empathy, compassion, courtesy, respect, responsibility, authenticity – along with the harder military ones of his calling. Every knight was a warrior, but not every warrior was a knight.

So the code originates from the days when a strong man with a sword could easily steal from you or kill you, or just take whatever he wanted by force. The idea of the code seems to be to formalise a better way of behaving, to limit violence to that in a good cause, to channel aggression and masculinity in a positive direction, to control and guide people who otherwise could just terrorise the landscape. In essence, it dealt with three basic but overlapping areas of a knight's duty: to his people, to his church, and to women. Honour loomed large in all these – it's for this reason that I have my own heraldic motto *Quid Triumphis Nisi Honeste*, or 'what use is victory without honour?' – but in many cases there was a heavy religious element too. Duties to his countrymen were framed more in terms of them being fellow Christians than those of other competing world religions, duties to the church involved submission to God as the final arbiter, and duties to women likewise placed Our Lady, the Virgin Mary, above all others. Arguably, though, actual knighthood, and tales of derring-do and epic adventures that get rolled into chivalric tales of King Arthur and his court, predate the introduction of Christianity to the west, as can be seen in the Nordic sagas. Their popularity was such that they became melded into the troubadors' and jongleurs' tales.

The modern sense of chivalry as associated with love was prevalent back then too, but in different ways. Love of one's fellow man was one of the Christian virtues, whether they be socially below you (in which case they needed to be protected) or socially above you (in which case they needed to be obeyed, particularly in the case of a knight and his lord, and even in this case unto death). Love of God was not just for the clergy and those in holy orders, but also for a Christian knight who saw himself as defending good from evil. The love of women was courtly love, in many tales unrequited or unobtainable, with the knight there to protect and admire his ladies without the expectation of sex or marriage.

Although knights were framed as heroic figures, strong on the battlefield, robust and true, at least as we understand the concept today, there is a difference between chivalry and heroism. Heroism was external, a response to outside pressures (most notably conflict, of course). Chivalry was internal, a way of living which came from deeply held values and applicable to even – or perhaps especially – the quietest moments in life. Heroism also tended to be communal, involving knights and/ or soldiers en masse, whereas chivalry was more individual and the questing involved more personal, often involving abstinence or self-control. Most of the Arthurian tales are about striving against worldly desires and weaknesses and trying, and mostly failing, to achieve goals, but continuing to try. Striving, failing and striving again is very chivalric.

So, what exactly does the Chivalric Code entail? This is a harder question to answer than it may appear, for one very good reason: there is no single definitive code, there never has been, though many codes have been written down, and still are. It's quite a nebulous concept, which is, ironically, part of chivalry itself. Several different ones have survived down the centuries, and obviously there's a decent amount of overlap between them, but there is no one set of rules to which you can point and say, 'This is the Chivalric Code.'

The French historian Leon Gautier formulated an overtly Biblical Ten Commandments of Chivalry:

1.   Thou shalt believe all that the Church teaches, and shalt observe all its directions

2. Thou shalt defend the Church
3. Thou shalt respect all weaknesses, and shalt constitute thyself the defender of them
4. Thou shalt love the country in which thou wast born
5. Thou shalt not recoil before thine enemy
6. Thou shalt make war against the Infidel without cessation, and without mercy
7. Thou shalt perform scrupulously thy feudal duties, if they be not contrary to the laws of God
8. Thou shalt never lie, and shall remain faithful to thy pledged word
9. Thou shalt be generous, and give largesse to everyone
10. Thou shalt be everywhere and always the champion of the Right and the Good against Injustice and Evil.

However, not only was Gautier writing near the end of the 19th century, hundreds of years after the knights of the chivalric age had been active, but many of his commandments are so explicitly religious to modern-day sensibilities – in the case of his sixth commandment, inflammatorily so – that they are of only limited use in helping us navigate our way through life as we know it.

The 11th century French epic poem *The Song of Roland*, whose protagonist was Emperor Charlemagne's nephew, lists a 17-point code:

1. To fear God and maintain His Church
2. To serve the liege lord in valour and faith
3. To protect the weak and defenceless
4. To give succour to widows and orphans
5. To refrain from the wanton giving of offence
6. To live by honour and for glory

7. To despise pecuniary reward
8. To fight for the welfare of all
9. To obey those placed in authority
10. To guard the honour of fellow knights
11. To eschew unfairness, meanness and deceit
12. To keep faith
13. At all times to speak the truth
14. To persevere to the end in any enterprise begun
15. To respect the honour of women
16. Never to refuse a challenge from an equal
17. Never to turn the back upon a foe

There is much more in this than in Gautier's list which is relevant today – point five, 'To refrain from the wanton giving of offence', should be plastered on the home page of every social media platform, given how toxic those places can get; and point eleven, 'To eschew unfairness, meanness and deceit', is always good advice for life – but there are still a couple of problematic areas. The first two points feel anachronistic, point seven ('To despise pecuniary reward') is unnecessarily self-abnegating (it's not money that's the root of all evil, after all, but the love of money: and money in itself is useful for all kinds of things), point nine doesn't take account of the many instances in which those in authority simply aren't up to the responsibility demanded of them, and point thirteen is laudable in principle but unworkable in practice (I believe very strongly in not lying, but there's a way from that to speaking the truth *at all times*).

So it's the list of virtues as outlined by the Duke of Burgundy in the 14th century – a couple of hundred years after *The Song of Roland* but still squarely in the heyday of the medieval knight – which are perhaps easiest to apply to modern life.

There are a dozen of them, simple enough to be universal but specific enough to resonate both then and now.

1. Faith
2. Charity
3. Justice
4. Sagacity
5. Prudence
6. Temperance
7. Resolution
8. Truth
9. Liberality
10. Diligence
11. Hope
12. Valour

What follows is how I see these twelve knightly pillars in modern life, and how I have tried to live my own life according to their tenets. I was going to say, 'my own life, both professional and personal', but for me there is no real delineation: I am one of the lucky people who loves what I do so much that I don't mark it as 'work' to delineate it from 'home'. I hope that you find it interesting, useful and applicable, whoever you are. The knights who originally followed this code were men, of course, but our society is so different that today's chivalric qualities can, and should be, applied to everyone irrespective of gender, colour, creed or political leaning. As Gandalf says in *The Lord of the Rings*, 'I have found that it is the small everyday deeds of ordinary folk that keep the darkness at bay. Small acts of kindness and love.' To be chivalric does not necessarily mean to fight great monsters and combat vast evil, it means to live decently and try to help others.

This book is neither a conventional biography, though there are of course biographical elements, nor specifically an instruction manual, but a bit of both. I have more than a dozen horses, though the one I'm most associated with is a white Lusitano called Warlord. A breed and type of horse that would have been much sought after in medieval England or France. I train my own warhorses every day, teaching them high school manoeuvres that can be seen so beautifully performed by the Spanish riding school, and ride out across the English countryside on the same steeds as well as actually jousting for fun and relaxation (yes, I'm aware that the traditional definition of 'relaxation' is being stretched to the limit here). I own several custom-made steel suits of armour, probably known as harnesses in medieval times, as a suit of armour is a phrase likely coined by the Victorians, who so loved the gothic, but who got so much of it wrong. I'm probably as well known for my Modern History YouTube channel, where I put up short films about any and all aspects of medieval life, as I am for my work in co-founding and co-running Rebellion, one of the more successful computer games companies on the planet. As one journalist who interviewed me said: 'To put it bluntly, there aren't many successful chief executives who can be seen on the internet swinging an axe at a watermelon.'

Nor is this book simply a repurposing of an ancient text to apply to the modern business world, as has been done with, say, Sun Tzu's *The Art of War* and Niccolo Machiavelli's *The Prince*. It's certainly less cynical than either of those, because in business the Chivalric Code means paying people on time, doing fair deals, protecting the weaker and less fortunate, and being a decent person: not a pushover or a goody-two-shoes, but someone who stands up for what's right. There are also some less structured and more random thoughts about the world, but most of all this book is, I hope, a testament to an area of history which I find endlessly fascinating and which gives me so much pleasure. Of course not all of the Chivalric Code will map neatly onto modern life. It didn't when it was invented, and doesn't now. To misquote a popular fictional pirate, 'They're more guidelines than rules.'

Chapter One

Faith

FOR MOST PEOPLE, the word 'faith' has religious or spiritual overtones: faith in a deity or a creed. Indeed faith is often defined as 'belief without evidence', the exact opposite of the scientific principle of knowledge. For medieval knights, such belief was a given: their world was not just a Christian one but sometimes aggressively so, waging conflicts in the name of the Lord (the fact that the other side as often as not was doing the same thing was rather by the by: and in any case, variations on 'my God is better than your God' have accounted for untold deaths throughout history).

But in our much more secular world, an explicitly religious faith can seem superfluous. I'm not an especially religious person myself. I'd love the supernatural to be real, just as I'd love ogres and dragons and unicorns to really exist. Well, they do exist in the mind, but most of them don't in the real physical world. Arguably the unicorn does actually exist though, just bigger, more stumpy and aggressive and is called the Rhinocerous. I think it quite likely that travellers' tales of that creature became changed into the deer or horse like creatures beloved of fantasy books and medieval tapestries alike. I love all of the good parts about religions: churches, cathedrals, temples, mosques, the spirit of community. Walking into a cathedral is always something special: the architecture, the beauty, the peace, the sunlight streaming through the stained glass windows, all never fail to move me. These are things built by man in God's name, and that combination is also a part of storytelling, the elevation from the ordinary by a higher power, the motivation to strive and create something vast and wonderful, but I hate the negativity that comes with the worst parts, and I loathe extremism of all forms, and the close-minded dogmatic ignorant individuals who live at the fringes of most dogmas.

Luckily, and even though medieval knights were all, at least on the surface, practising Christians, the word 'faith' in the Chivalric Code did not have religious connotations. Chivalric faith meant fidelity rather than spirituality. It meant trust and integrity, a pledge to always be faithful to one's promises no matter how big or small they were, and that's a lesson which is equally applicable today. Keeping faith also means to battle onwards, no matter how hard the path is: to believe in yourself and those around you, to maintain your ambitions, get up if knocked down, to persist with your quest, remain honest to yourself about what you're trying to achieve, to strive towards your goals and hope that your visions will succeed. In many ways, faith is what makes us work hard and progress: we need to believe that what we're doing is worthwhile if we are really to enjoy our work.

I feel this very strongly. I've not always had faith in myself, but I've always tried to have faith within me, and I always hoped I'd get to where I am and beyond. I always wanted to work for myself and maintained the faith that I would be successful on that journey. I didn't really focus just on the end goal, as that always shifts away like the horizon, but on the doing, on the quest itself and the steps needed to find the Grail. I love exploring the frontier of technology, which combined with entertainment is always an exciting area. For me at Rebellion, my faith is that we are in our own small way making the world a better place. Obviously we're not finding cures for cancer or anything of screamingly obvious social benefit, but what we do brings a lot of people across the globe a lot of pleasure, and that's not to be sniffed at. We give those who play our games the chance to lose themselves in the worlds we create for long periods at a time, we help foster a sense of community among our game players, and we allow our teams to explore their creativity and talents.

These are all things which make us human, which allow us to live rather than just to exist. It annoys me when the arts, in whatever form, are seen as an afterthought, an optional extra bolted onto the more serious business of life itself. If there were no arts, what would life be like? No books, no films, no TV programmes, no music, no video games, no paintings, no sculptures, no plays, no musicals, no opera, no ballet... It would be a pretty monochrome existence, because even if you don't like all or even most of those categories you're bound to like some of them.

One of my own articles of faith is the importance of storytelling for humans. My interest in storytelling, particularly as part of games, goes all the way back to childhood. My brother Chris and I grew up in Osgathorpe, Leicestershire, right on the edge of what had in olden times been the Danelaw, the wiggly and blurred line that marked out the early medieval border agreed by Alfred and Guthrum in the late ninth century. Our dad was a doctor and our mum a teacher, so we had a nice solid sensible upbringing. We grew up playing on early computers – our first bought computer was a Commodore PET in the late 1970s which our parents had saved up to buy, as it was the equivalent of a couple of grand in those days – and at the time it felt like *Star Trek*, allowing us to boldly go to frontiers we'd only previously dreamed about. Our actual first computer was an Edukit built from parts by my brother Chris. (By modern standards, of course, the commodore PET is risibly limited, but then again forty years from now all our current state-of-the-art technology will seem just as antediluvian to our descendants as those early PCs do to us.)

We also loved board games. At the age of eight I wanted to make Monopoly more exciting, so I invented Nuclear Monopoly. Not only could you buy houses and hotels and all that kind of stuff, but you could also buy nuclear missiles (which were actually wooden pegs). You could buy one-dice, two-dice or three-dice-strong nuclear missiles and you could shoot them at other people. You'd nominate one of your properties as a launch site then roll the dice, move the missile and blow up what was on the landing square, reducing it back down to zero. If somebody had a hotel there you could try to nuke them and take it away, though the randomness of the dice roll meant that you might nuke one of your own properties, perhaps foreshadowing mutually assured destruction as a concept in the real world. It was the Cold War, after all: a time when schoolkids were shown how to hide under desks in case of a nuclear blast, when public buildings had sirens with different codes for attack warnings and fallout risk, and when now and then tensions between the USA and USSR spilled over and the fear of planetary annihilation would become briefly but scarily real. Still, I didn't realise quite how dark my idea was. At the time it was just a variation to make the game go for even longer and cause even more upset about money.

But we weren't inactive, indoor kids, hissing like vampires if the curtains were drawn. We rode ponies, explored disused farmhouses, got caught on railway lines, fell into streams. I'd wear wellies and tramp up in the stream, seeing how long I could keep the inside of my boots dry before getting what I'd call a 'wet socker'. It seemed a long way that I went, not just upstream but also down one field and across another, though in reality it was probably no more than a quarter mile, half a mile tops. I'd take a backpack with sandwiches and crisps, eat them at the limit point I'd set beforehand, and then turn back. Even then I was formulating narratives and setting parameters with a view to improving the experience: making myself walk in the water rather than alongside the stream, creating mental landscapes, making up small adventures for myself (and my pony when I took one along, on which occasions I fancied myself some sort of Leicestershire child version of a knight errant), and so on. I thought of this small patch of the countryside as virgin, unexplored wilderness, even though it had been mapped to within an inch of its life: but to me it hadn't, and so these stories unfurled themselves in front of me like a medieval scroll full of endless promise. Places I visited were given names, the old waterfall, the haunted shed, the place of the skull (I found a bird skull), the swing tree (there was an old rope there), the great marsh (about 40 square feet of boggy ground caused by a blocked drain, probably).

I went through a traditional, high-level education, so I did O-levels and A-levels and then went on to St. John's, Oxford, to read zoology with my tutor Tom Kemp. But I don't remember ever not being into games. All that time I kept making up ideas, modifying games for other people, and making up places and landscapes for people to explore. At school I was really into fantasy adventures like Dungeons and Dragons and other role-playing games, most notably Tunnels and Trolls, with its famous tongue-in-cheek attack spell TTYF (take that you fiend) which I used to play with friends during a lunchtime club. It's quite funny, thinking of the *Stranger Things* TV show, because that was me. I was there, and I knew all that. I was one of the first people I knew who played role playing games. I bought first edition copies of everything and I managed to persuade a teacher to lend us one of the store cupboards with a table in it, so we could continue the adventure each school lunchtime. We'd each take on a fantasy character, such as a wizard or knight; I almost always played a paladin, go figure, and then throw dice to determine how the characters interacted with each other and how the stories developed.

Then, in my first year at university, I wrote a couple of adventure game books for Ladybird. They weren't conventionally structured like 'normal' books: they involved the reader making choices for themselves rather than simply following a predetermined narrative. For example, section 7 of *Steeleye and the Lost Magic* reads, 'Further on, the way is strewn with small pebbles and different colours. Then the path divides. On one of the paths there are black and white pebbles. The other is covered with smooth green grass. If you choose the pebbly path, turn to section 12: if you choose the grassy path, turn to 60.' This was of course a rather simplistic version of computer game narratives, which are by necessity much more complex, but in essence it's the same thing. Of course, as so often in life (and business), a strength can also be a weakness, and what made these adventure books so appealing was also one of the problems with them: that you could decide to make a choice, and if you turned one way or the other you could always go back. I thought that was unfair. (As an aside, it's noticeable in those Ladybird adventure books that all the colour is in the middle ground and that the wrong paths, the extremes on both sides, are black and white: an early if unconscious example of my distaste for extremism.)

People often ask me what my best preparation for business was, and I think, genuinely, that it was a good general academic education in the basics. How to construct an argument, how to think through a problem, how to try to avoid biases and cognitive fallacies as best you can, how to avoid deciding until you've gathered evidence, how to say 'I don't know' and look it up later. My fascination, love and respect for animals and science was what led me to study zoology (there was no such thing as a computer games degree in those days), and it has helped in every area of what I do now as it taught me how to analyse data and statistics, solve problems and also not to necessarily take people at their word, especially if they don't provide any evidence, or refuse to listen to facts. A zoology degree was quite a broad education in processes and systems, a much wider area of study than 'just animals' as one of my student colleagues joked. A biological entity, a living being, is in many ways parallel to that of a business. You have a central nervous system co-ordinating everything, muscles and guts doing a lot of work, some of it literally shitty. The brain is the management, both consciously and unconsciously sending signals everywhere; it all needs to be linked by nerves or internal communications and it's run according to some simple rules.

I was lucky in my timing, with computer technology coming of age more or less as I did. But by the late '80s the technology had caught up with our ambitions (not that computer manufacturers gave two hoots what a couple of Oxford graduates thought, but anyway). It was around the time I needed to start thinking of what I was going to do after completing my academic studies. I'd followed my undergraduate zoology degree with a DPhil (Oxford's equivalent to most other places' PhD) on wildlife conservation, studying with the Wildlife Conservation Unit led by David Macdonald, which I did for two years, but I became too distracted with everything else that was going on and developing and never completed my thesis. Maybe I'll go back and finish it one day. Chris, who'd studied chemistry at Wadham College, Oxford, also began a doctorate, but his went the same way as mine. Once the research was done, the writing up was relatively boring. Our parents weren't especially happy about our career choice, and perhaps understandably so: they had two bright sons who could have found good proper jobs in any number of scientific or professional arenas, and here we are messing around with unproven technology making what must have seemed to them like frivolous games.

Chris was more technical, very involved with programming and technology, and I was more into computer art, games design and writing, so making video games together seemed a very natural progression. We started off keying in the games shared as listings in monthly magazines, then began trying to computerise adventure game books, and from there moved into actual game development. One summer we stayed in Oxford and I worked for one of the local games companies, Oxford Digital Enterprises. I was living in a house on the Cowley Road belonging to Gideon Amos, who was at what was then Oxford Poly and is now a big cheese in the Lib Dems, and there was quite a kerfuffle when one of his other housemates, who was treasurer of the student union, did a runner to South America with about £200k or so. It would be a lot of money even now, but back then it was an almost unimaginable amount, especially when you were used to living on student budgets. Oxford Digital Enterprises commissioned us to do *The Hunt for Red October*, based on the hit book and movie about a Russian nuclear sub which defects to the USA, and for Mirrorsoft I created, designed and did all the art for the fantasy game *Blade Warrior*. Mirrorsoft was owned by Robert Maxwell, who, if you remember, was found drowned at sea, with various lurid tales of whether it was suicide; or was he murdered? All I knew was that he owed me quite a few tens of thousands of pounds for the success of *Blade Warrior*. I never got the money.

Although at that stage I was just a freelance artist, I found myself increasingly being roped into wrangling other people to work on projects with me: and then, since I was efficient and conscientious, I soon became a de facto producer on the games I was working on. But I was still being paid only as an artist, so this seemed a mug's game. If I was going to be a producer then I wanted to have both the remuneration and control the job merited, and the only way to be sure of that was to set up on our own. Chris was keen too, so we looked up how to form a limited company and started Rebellion. We were going to be called Revolution, but found out at the eleventh hour there already was one, owned and run by Charles Cecil who we later got to know as a colleague and friend.

We took the inspiration for our logo from Solidarnosc, the Polish trade union Solidarity which had become famous in the West during the Cold War for standing up to the communist government there. We were very inspired by their typeface, not just because it suited the image we had of ourselves but also because the Solidarnosc logo was burned in the collective memory of those who'd lived through the Cold War: it was iconic both politically and as a part of pop culture. But it was also pure and simple, made a great logo. Most of our customers today are way too young to remember Solidarnosc or its leader Lech Walesa, a shipyard electrician from Gdansk who would later become Poland's president (looking back now I realise he was only in his late thirties when he became globally famous, even though he looked about twenty years older than that): but our logo is still as distinctive as ever even when shorn from its original.

The name 'Rebellion' said it all. We felt that, a bit like in the music industry in the early days, the people making the money weren't the people who were actually making the product. It was the people commissioning or selling the product who were getting wealthy and we wanted to break that mould. The hard part was coming up with ideas and making them happen. So, with the hubris of youth, our name was running a flag up to say we plan to be different. Right from the very earliest days together, we wanted to do things in a non-standard way. We wanted to do things our way because we thought we'd make better games that way. We were the upstarts, the new kids on the block, and we weren't going to follow the path more trodden. There were adventures to be had in places no-one had been before.

One of the first games we developed as Rebellion in the early '90s was for Atari, which had once been huge but by then was a shadow of its former self. From being one of the fastest growing companies ever and a global entertainment behemoth, perhaps similar to giants like Facebook or Google, it had made some bad decisions, had some bad luck and shrunk to a much smaller scale. We went into these huge offices in Slough and they obviously hadn't been renovated in quite a while. They had brown hessian wallpaper, threadbare on the corners where thousands of corporate hands had rubbed through to the backing sheets. It was very 1970s, classically, achingly so. Like something from a sitcom set back then. I was dressed in jeans and T-shirt as usual. Those days the jeans were Levi 501s, inspired by that brilliant advert starring Nick Cave in boxers in a laundrette. These days I tend to wear Wranglers. Why you may ask? Well it's because of the seams. Wranglers have the thin seam on the inside of the leg, which is what you need for riding horses as it's much more comfortable. Business executives of a certain type usually like to dress a certain way because that's the uniform which they think projects competence, confidence and importance. I couldn't care less. I'm very rarely seen in a suit and tie. As far as I'm concerned, suits and ties are for weddings, funerals and possibly meeting royalty, only.

We had prepared a demo of a game where dragons fought Viking longships, and we showed it to a few people there, including the managing director Bob Gleadow. A demo is a small fraction of a game that's designed to show people what the final game might be like. A demo needs to be impactful and interesting to work, which ours was.

'This is absolutely perfect for our new Jaguar console,' Bob said.

'What new Jaguar console?' said everyone else in the room who worked for Atari at the time.

It turned out that this was the first they'd all heard of a new console, so in a way this was their official internal announcement. As you can imagine, there was quite a lot of confusion as people tried to make sense of it, and quite a few noses put out of joint too, so the conversation was quite strained as they sorted it out – and all the time Chris and I were standing there awkwardly feeling like bystanders at someone else's family row. When the dust had settled we'd been commissioned to make two games: *Checkered Flag*, a 3D racing game, and *Aliens vs. Predator*, which mashed up the creatures from the Alien and Predator movie franchises. Though we'd created *Aliens vs. Predator*, the rights belonged to 20th Century Fox Studios. The idea came from a love of the original films, which we thought would be cool to combine, and as far as I know we were the first people to think of that. It would be another decade before the film of the same name came out, hugely inspired by our work on the game.

People look at Rebellion now and see that we have various strings to our bow, with computer games and publishing, movie studios, comic books and board games, but deep down they come back to the same thing: storytelling in one form or another. Many of the skills people have in different parts of the media are transferable precisely because of this, though many are not and some might seem to be applicable, but really aren't. We'd been creating our own games with original ideas, ideas from others and ideas from movies, but we were always interested in looking at other forms of storytelling. I'd been a weekly reader of that stalwart of the British comics scene, *2000 AD*, home of Judge Dredd, since 1977. Happily, after a lot of behind the scenes work, our first major acquisition was buying *2000 AD* in, appropriately enough, the year 2000 (which if nothing else makes the date of purchase easy to remember). I've often been asked whether this was a business decision or one which came from love of the comic and its iconic characters, and it was a mix of both. We wouldn't have been able to do it if it hadn't been a good business decision. It was valuable intellectual property, or IP, there was an obvious potential for cross-pollination of games and comics (our *Rogue Trooper* game received BAFTA nominations for Best Character and Best Screenplay in 2006), and we felt there were lots of areas where we could do business from it: games, books, collectible figurines, and so on. It also needed rebuilding as far as we were concerned.

Equally I don't think we'd have been interested in doing it if it hadn't been a passion and something that needed to be done. Business for me isn't just about numbers, though numbers are important, but about people and ideas. So that split between business and passion wasn't quite 50/50: it was skewed towards passion. *2000 AD* needed to be rescued, it needed to be reinvigorated and I felt it very important for British culture as well that it didn't die on its arse. We felt that *2000 AD* was in decline, lacking investment under its then current owner (one of several hands it had passed through over the years), and needed to be owned and cherished by someone who knew the culture of what it was trying to do and cared about the writing and artwork. I genuinely think it is an important bit of our national cultural heritage, and we wanted to use the money we'd earned from games to make a heartfelt and uncynical acquisition in the traditional publishing sector. At heart the decision was because *2000 AD* was all about great storytelling and great world building, and it was that which had captured me as a child when I'd read the very first issue back in 1977, bought from a newsagent whilst carrying a very hot bag of vinegary chips from the chippy next door, which for some reason I remember as being called The 300 Spartans. Why a chip shop in a Leicestershire town should have been named after the legendary battle of Thermopylae is still a conundrum. Having said that, the world would be a better place if all fish and chip shops were named after great battles.

We also have a book publishing arm, with several imprints. Originally Abaddon Books, and now Solaris and Solaris Worlds, which publishes many original novels a year, including ones set in the aftermath of a global plague (bonus points for prescience), on an alien world to which a company of World War I soldiers have been inexplicably transported, and a steampunk alternate history in which Queen Victoria, by now over 160 years old, still governs the British Empire towards the end of the 20th century. These series didn't come from existing IP. As Abaddon editor Jonathan Oliver said, 'It's a really odd model. It's franchise fiction without a franchise. We're giving writers the spark of an idea and asking, "Can you do this?" But we're not giving them an idea that is based on a game or a film, or anything... We're just saying: "Wouldn't it be cool if this kind of fiction existed? Could you write this kind of fiction for us?" No one else has ever really done this, used the franchise model in that way. They've always had a product and the book was the sub-product. We knew we wanted to publish genre fiction. We sat down and thought, well, we can't just publish one series, we've got to have different flavours for different readers – attract the widest readership possible. It was as simple as saying: we want science fiction, we want fantasy, we want horror. Our stuff is accessible to everyone and I think the market for genre books is really wide. All we do is try to tell the best stories we can in the genre.'

As a result, along with the acquisition of the old IPC comic library, which dates back to the very origin and birth of the word 'comic', in the 1880s' *Comic Cuts for Boys*, we now have a catalogue that is arguably deeper and richer than Marvel's, with more varied stories. People laugh when I say that, but it's true. It's not about comparing the respective commercial fortunes of Marvel and us, because clearly they win that by a long way, but so much of their stuff is quite narrow superhero stories, and leads to what some people say are cookie-cutter movies where some absurdly-figured superhero, with magical powers, in tight Lycra is bemoaning his or her fate. Our library, though less well known, covers far more concepts, and that makes me proud and happy as it means we can appeal to a wider audience: again, not necessarily a larger one, but one with more varied tastes. With Marvel, if you don't like superheroes you're largely out of luck. With us, there's something in our very deep back catalogue that will resonate with you no matter how esoteric your tastes.

Even romance novels, we have a load of picture magazines filled with chaste romantic tales, plus volumes of historical works, including one World War II era comic on how to set ambushes for Nazis if you are a schoolboy with a rifle. Seriously.

Half the fun is playing around with those different genres, be it in books, comics or video games. Take *Strange Brigade*, a game where you the player are one of a team of eccentric 1930s adventurers. Their world is very much based on the adventure serials of that decade, which in turn inspired and influenced Steven Spielberg when he was doing Indiana Jones. I said to my team, 'Don't lift from Indiana Jones, be inspired by the original adventure stories. Go back to the source, to the primary data.' We're obviously influenced by everything in our current culture but I don't want to derive our work from those things. I want us to go back to the source material. Go back to the Saturday matinee pictures. Poke fun at our own culture, our British culture. Stiff upper lip and all that, we play around with that. A little bit of self-parody is healthy. And we need some humour in things at the moment with the way the world is going.

Nostalgia is a valuable flavour to add to the pallet of our storytelling, because it taps into that sense of the stories we shape from our own lives, and particularly from those times in our lives when things felt so powerful and emotional:

childhood, schooldays, teenage years, the university years, when every day was a new experience, when life was about discovery, and when friendships were so intense. This is why remake projects are so popular on new consoles: games design doesn't age quickly, but graphics, resolution and user interface do. Also, supposedly it mitigates risk as the previous title was a success; the theory goes that the remake will do the same. When we recently remastered *Rogue Trooper*, we found that the gameplay was rock solid and fantastic, but the graphics needed to be updated for today's consumer. There's a lot to be said for that kind of repackaging and putting excellent gameplay into a shiny new box. I'm sure that gameplay does age, just more slowly than other aspects of the games industry.

Humans not only need stories, and to learn from them, but they also prefer them to be told in particular ways, ways which maximise our psychological and emotional response to them. The best storytelling engages us at a very deep level and transports us to other places and always has done, from the first rhythmic storytelling around an open fire, to the photons leaving the screen of our visual display units, the medium is not as important as the tale. There is a pervasive idea around storytelling, that of the monomyth. A kind of fundamental core of any story, so the theory goes (though sometimes I wonder if anything could be distilled like this; after all, sport of all sorts could be simplified to people competing with each other to win and following some game rules). The monomyth concept is that any story involving a hero and their journey is fundamentally the same irrespective of cultural or historical influences. In his book *The Hero with a Thousand Faces*, the American professor of literature Joseph Campbell described this fundamental narrative pattern (as he describes it) as, 'A hero ventures forth from the world of common day into a region of supernatural wonder: fabulous forces are there encountered and a decisive victory is won: the hero comes back from this mysterious adventure with the power to bestow boons on his fellow man.'

Campbell went so far as to break down the journey into three separate sections – departure, initiation and return – with each section further broken down into stages (five for departure and six each for initiation and return to make seventeen in all). Other writers have formulated different stages, but they all tend to agree on the existence of the three main sections. *Departure* involves the hero's ordinary existence being disrupted by a call to adventure, which he is usually reluctant to accept and/or may need to be helped by a mentor figure. *Initiation* involves the hero crossing an actual or metaphorical threshold to a new world where he faces tasks or trials, again either alone or in company, until he reaches the crux of his quest where in order to triumph he must overcome an enemy or obstacle greater than any before, and in doing so reach new heights in his own personal qualities (the kind of qualities demanded by the Chivalric Code, appropriately enough). Lastly *Return* involves his journey back to the ordinary world, sometimes in haste while being pursued by antagonists from the other world or perhaps as reluctantly as he came if he has grown to love this world. He has been transformed by his adventure and is a better person and warrior for it.

We use this, or perhaps parts of it, in many of our computer games, as does the industry in general one way or another. (I discuss what goes into making a computer game in more detail in the *Diligence* chapter.) The beats are not always exactly the same, but the baseline is always there if you look hard enough. And the very nature of computer games also makes explicit the conflation between hero and player. Many games are partly wish fulfilment after all. You too can be a famous racing driver, a valiant hero, a super soldier, a mighty wizard or even a criminal mastermind. Since many games are played from a first person point-of-view, in which the action is seen through the eyes of the main character, the player is literally the hero in his or her own narrative. There are, of course, other styles of viewpoint in games: the third person one, in which you hover, puppet-master-like behind and usually above the main character, or bird's eye view, usually reserved for games where you are some being in overall command of many entities in the game world, which is also sometimes called god's eye view. (As an aside you might notice I've skipped from first person to third person. I'm not actually sure how a *second* person view game might turn out, or, in fact, what that sort of game view might be.) In the world of the video game, everything else melts away: it's often the purest escapism, not just because you're immersed in a new world (what I've always wanted is to create landscapes for people to explore, and almost all of our games are landscapes with games overlaid) but also because you are the main player in that world rather than simply a passive observer. In the many *Sniper Elite* games we've made over the years, for example, you aren't yourself with all your everyday problems: bills to pay, a job you're bored by, relationship issues, the need to go to the toilet at intervals or even grab a decent night's sleep. You're a highly skilled, highly focussed special forces long-distance killing machine, doing something which has been baked deep into human DNA by millennia of fighting, killing the enemy well. That's a very seductive scenario which most of us will hopefully never have to experience in real life at all. Real life soldiering, if the many memoirs are to be believed, is a combination of ninety-nine percent discomfort and boredom and one percent abject terror. We've spoken to many real life soldiers whilst doing our research for the *Sniper Elite* titles, and one thing that we've always decided to leave out of our games of particular and quite unsanitary, but amusingly unheroic note, is that the real sniper needs to poo in a plastic bag for days whilst stalking the target.

Interestingly, some of the most popular franchises in movie and literary history have more or less followed this pattern, at least in one important way. Knowing that readers and viewers will mentally insert themselves in the role of protagonist, those protagonists are by accident or design often rendered bland and ordinary, as if their magnolia tones will enable the viewer to map many of their own aspects onto the on-screen persona. George Lucas has repeatedly admitted the influence of the monomyth on *Star Wars*, so Luke Skywalker is a good example, as are Harry Potter, Tintin and Asterix. In each case the main character is actually pretty much a blank canvas. They display basic positive qualities – they're brave, they're loyal, they're intelligent – but they don't display much, if anything, by way of contradiction or depth of character.

Why? Because they don't need to. They are, for the purposes of the narrative, a blank canvas onto which the reader or viewer can project themselves. And, crucially, the supporting characters in each of those franchises are magnificently rich and varied. To take just three from each of them: Darth Vader, Han Solo and Chewbacca; Hagrid, Albus Dumbledore and Severus Snape; Captain Haddock, Cuthbert Calculus and the Thompson Twins; and Obelix, Getafix and Vitalstatistix. These are all memorable characters, richly layered and endlessly watchable/readable. (On a tangential note, talking of epic storytelling, *Lord of the Rings* fans may be amused to know that in the comments on my YouTube channel, I'm occasionally likened to the movie portrayal of Boromir's dad

Denethor.) And even what we think of as ancient classics today were at the time of writing often seen as anything but: both *Magna Carta* and the *Divine Comedy* were written as a form of revenge, and indeed Dante spends most of the *Inferno* dreaming up ever more gruesome punishments for his enemies in medieval Florence.

Actually, however, my own view of faith in the wider sense goes exactly the other way: not worrying too much about what our competitors are doing. We don't really care what other people do with their games because what we care about is what we do with our games and what our players think of them. They could do games any way they like in any different way they want to. They can spend as much money or as little money as suits them, and if the games are great I'll play them and if they're not I don't really care. We've never been deliberately isolationist or deliberately different. As much as our name would say we want to do things differently, we just want to do things our way and make good stuff. And since we produce the kind of games we want to play, we have been able at times to ride the waves of industry controversy without getting swept up in them. If you copy what other people are doing, you're by necessity behind them. Sometimes that doesn't matter to the audience at all, we've had more than a few of our innovative games copied in parts by others, and the audience neither notices nor cares, which is a little frustrating, but a good lesson in life.

New business models turn up at regular intervals if you're in any industry for long enough. Take the whole loot box issue, where games are free to play usually, but not always, and include what have come to be known as 'loot boxes'. The key feature of loot boxes is that, like a lucky dip, you pay real money and take a chance. You might get something useful, you might not. Repeat until you get what you want. It's according to many a classic addictive loop called operant conditioning, made famous by the work of Professor Skinner at Harvard University in the 1960s. These mechanisms come in for a lot of criticism on the grounds that they were part of compulsion loops engineered into games to keep players hooked, with possible ramifications for those players both in terms of game addiction and financial distress, which in some few cases can be a very bad thing. Many people can control this addictive loop, but some cannot. The biggest argument against loot boxes is that they are available to children and the vulnerable and, unlike traditional gambling, not hedged about with legislation. At Rebellion we've dabbled in free to play and had a moderate amount of success in it, though never touched on the random reward feature. I think it would be much more fun if the mechanism was called 'Skinners' or 'Skinning', as there's something Science Fictiony about the term. I can imagine it being used in *Blade Runner*. Or as one executive defending the phenomenon in front of members of Parliament in a Select Committee that I attended said, 'We prefer to call it surprise mechanics.' It was not well received. Fundamentally we prefer to make traditional action- and narrative-driven games with a multiplayer component. We managed to avoid all the loot box controversy because we just don't do them in our games. I'm a huge believer in single player games so while I'm in charge, we're going to keep making single player games alongside exploring new and emerging ways of interacting with the virtual world. Personally I'm unpracticed and disappointingly rubbish at multiplayer games, particularly PvP (player versus player) games, and even more particularly if I'm ever identified. I usually choose to play multiplayer games incognito, unless I have a good reason to be the target.

Storytelling is at heart escape: to take yourself out of your own place in space and time and plonk you down somewhere else. This is why I love medieval horsemanship and riding through the English countryside. It's a form of escape, adventure and even time travel. Although I was an experienced rider, having ridden competitively since I was eight years old, and competed at international level in dressage and show jumping, I didn't really get into medieval horsemanship in a big dedicated way until 2005, when Chris took me to an English Heritage event. There were historical re-enactors wearing armour, riding horses and jousting, and I was just captivated. Lots of ideas I'd had over the years dropped into place. My love of riding one handed with a stick in my right hand pretending to be a sword, which got me into so much trouble in Pony Club. Some of the reasons are obvious – here was something which combined my love of horses with that of other worlds – but it was also more than that. It was something visceral and atavistic, something which stirred things deep inside me. I just knew that this is what I wanted to do. And now, many years and a lot of experience on, I know what it feels like to close your visor in the heat of summer, pick up a lance and gallop past somebody at the very Tower of London, trying to hit them. I know what real jousting is like in the moat at Kenilworth Castle, I've ridden up Senlac Hill towards the line of worthy Huscarls defending England's last Anglo Saxon King, Harold Godwinson. It's a whole different window into a way of being a warrior which has died out. When you put on that authentic armour, made by hand of real steel, carry historical weapons (though blunted for safety usually) and sit astride a living horse, you are experiencing a lot of the same physical feedback as a person from way back then. Maybe not the fear of death, or the worry about how you might fight, but much of it, including the smells and sweat sometimes: in other words, you're time-travelling, or as close to it as we're ever likely to get.

The more you travel away from your own time and space, the more you see not just the differences between those worlds and yours but also the similarities too: or, perhaps more precisely, the way things transform, change, yet somehow also stay the same over time. For example, what is a modern-day corporate logo if not a contemporary version of the heraldic symbol: your group's standard in the battlefield of business? Heraldry was all about contrast and visibility and sending signals to your fellow warriors and the enemy too, especially once helmets with face protection came in following the years after 1066 (the medieval heraldic symbol also ensured co-ordination of colours between the various parts of battle regalia, such as the shield and the horse's armour, to prove who you were on the battlefield). Corporate logos perform the same function: the good ones stand out instantly. Both of them are branding: how you identify, what you value in your own personality, attributes and history, what you want to show off about, and all this in turn comes back to storytelling.

When noble families were joined by marriage, their coats of arms could also be joined and quartered, just as a corporate merger these days can result in an altogether new company with a new logo and corporate identity. Importance is itself important: heralds represented the king; therefore, if you attacked the herald then effectively you attacked the crown itself. The rules became ever more complex as time went by until heraldry was effectively its own set of enforceable laws, with its own judges and courts. You may be surprised to know that it still is. There is an heraldic court in London, called the College of Heralds that still convenes when necessary and there's one in Scotland, the fabulously named Court of the Lord Lyon.

Both still grant and administer all things heraldic. You might not have made the connection but the three lions (technically leopards, which is a medieval herald's joke, leo passant regardent, shortened to leo..pa..ard, get it?) that the English football team use is the same symbol that would have adorned the chest of King Richard Leoncourt, more usually known as The Lionheart. Those themselves come from the two lions of the Dukes of Normandy. History is embedded in our symbols. Surprisingly perhaps, even illegitimate sons could be marked on heraldry (and by name: the prefix 'Fitz' means 'bastard'), not through shame but simply through a device that's known as a 'difference'. One of several types of symbols that are placed over the arms of the father, which seem to go all the way down to the eighth son. Legitimacy meant church and property, so an illegitimate son would not inherit, but simply by virtue of his parentage he was deemed powerfully connected and very possibly showing some of his father's knightly qualities too.

The flipside of authenticity in branding is, of course, counterfeiting. The Ulfberht swords, made between the 9th and 11th centuries at a time when sword technology was passing from the Viking type to the later medieval type, also spawned one of the earliest examples we know of brand faking, yes real dodgy Viking knock-off swords, so we think. The genuine article cost a fortune and was made from the very best steel to ensure that it was, quite literally, a cut above the rest: but there were also some that were cheap knock-offs, in the modern parlance, often with the brand name spelt incorrectly! Today's equivalent would probably be a poorly-executed Nike swoosh on a pair of trainers or a counterfeit Tommy Hilfinger (sic) top in the local market.

Storytelling exists on a social level too. Each culture tells themselves certain things about what they value and what they don't. The vast majority of English people, for example, would recoil if you suggested that they eat dog or horse meat. This is a socio-cultural reflex – there's no nutritional reason not to eat either of those two animals if you also eat, for example, cows, chickens, sheep, and so on – and comes from a place in the collective psyche which says that, since dogs and horses are intelligent, we shouldn't eat them. (It's an inconsistent application to say the least: people eat pigs, which are also intelligent, and octopi, which are even more so.) But other cultures have no such strictures, as you can see in any East Asian street market. Eating horseflesh was a rite of passage among pagan tribes, since horses were seen as gifts from gods and consumed after they had fallen in battle. That medieval knights didn't do similar, unless they were in extremis, was because by that time the Catholic church had condemned it as a pagan (therefore non-Christian and borderline evil) ritual. Sometimes though we do have occasional records of those besieged holding out by eating their warhorses one by one until none were left, but it was the exception rather than the rule.

Although my industry is all about storytelling, I feel that – perhaps ironically – it's subject to misrepresentation both from without and within. The gaming industry is huge: at around £5 billion per annum, it's worth more than music and film combined, and is a pivotal export industry with games sold around the world (especially in markets which are resistant to many other export sectors). It's the fastest growing area of the creative economy, which is itself the fastest growing area of the British economy. But because very few people who work in the media really know, respect or understand computer games, the extent and importance of its cultural reach goes woefully under-reported. Specialist gaming media aside, you could be forgiven for thinking that video games are just a minority activity enjoyed by a few sad sacks in bedsits rather than what they actually are – an incredibly vibrant and creative sector full of dedicated and skilful designers and consumers. In fact, most mainstream reporting of the industry seems to be sensationalist moral panic stuff about the rotting of young people's brains and incitement to real-life violence, using a 'latest study' as the news hook and reporting its findings rather selectively, to say the least.

In fairness, this reluctance to accept computer games' rightful place in society comes from within the sector itself too. The entire retitling of 'e-sports' seems to me to be unproductive and reeks of a collective lack of self-confidence. What's wrong with calling them computer games? 'E-sports' is just social camouflage. They're not sport, not really. Sport, in my opinion, should be physically demanding, requiring fitness, co-ordination and strength, and though you won't find a greater champion of computer games than me, you also won't find me banging the drum for them to be considered a sport. I get the rationale behind it – the very physical prowess which the word 'sport' implies allows gamers to ally themselves with those whose physical gifts make them socially venerated – but I still think it's basically a theft of someone else's valour, some verbal legerdemain, in the same way that 'the cloud' gives the impression of something free floating, untethered and environmentally friendly rather than other people's computers in a warehouse consuming vast quantities of electricity.

The wider question of what makes a sport has long vexed even supposedly great minds. At Oxford, sports are divided into full blue and half blue status, depending on how important they are deemed in the life of the university and how much they demand from the participants. People laugh that ballroom dancing was deemed a half blue sport, but ballroom dancing is only a joke to those who've never tried it: and if *Strictly Come Dancing* has done anything, it has surely helped show that the professional dancers at least are serious athletes. One of my sports whilst I was at Oxford, riding, only qualified as a half blue, though as captain of the British student riding team I was awarded a full blue, excitingly and glamorously called an 'extraordinary' full blue – and even then there were a handful who tried to claim that it wasn't a sport at all. Not a sport? It's in the bloody Olympics!

All these, then, come under the topic of faith. Because it encompasses so much, it's rightly the first on the Duke of Burgundy's list: arguably, in fact, all the other qualities stem from this one, in the same way that 'pride' is listed first in the traditional seven deadly sins as all the other sins stem in one way or another from that.

Chapter Two

Charity

Like faith, charity is another virtue whose specific meaning in our society is not necessarily how medieval knights understood the concept. We think of charity primarily as giving – usually money, but also time and effort – to causes involving those less fortunate than ourselves, such as those suffering from poverty, illness, neglect or abuse in one form or another. In this respect I try to do my bit. Through the company we give money and time every year to SpecialEffect, a charity which helps people with special needs access and play computer games. I've also been giving money to Unicef my whole adult life. When I was a student I set up a direct debit for a few quid a month. It's scaled up since then.

I was a trustee at the Royal Armouries, an unpaid position which involves managing Her Majesty's Collection of Arms and Armour. The main collection is in a modern building in Leeds, alongside some docks, but there are components in the Tower of London, and some artillery in Portsmouth. It's a charitable organisation that looks after the Royal Armouries museum, and I gave my expertise each month for nothing. I'm also chair and founder of TIGA, a trade body for the games industry, and I do that for nothing too. I pick and choose carefully what I give my time and money to, because I think it's important to give to causes which really move you or to which you have a connection, not just because they're popular or fashionable, and certainly not because it might offer you some sort of material advantage such as tax relief or personal publicity.

But for a knight, charity meant something else – not something totally different, as the concept of giving to and looking after those less fortunate was very much part of the Chivalric Code, but certainly something more than just that. Just as the word 'chivalry' came from old French, so did the word 'charity': in this case from 'charité', which was itself derived from the Latin 'caritas', which was in turn a translation of the Greek word 'agape' (ἀγάπη), meaning unconditional love. In this definition, charity is not just the simple emotion of love but the expression of it too through actions rather than words, the seeking of the best for others. It was one of the seven Christian cardinal virtues, the opposite of the deadly sins: Thomas Aquinas considered it 'the most excellent of the virtues' and said that, 'The habit of charity extends not only to the love of God, but also to the love of our neighbour.' In other words, charity is basically God's love for humanity and humanity's love for each other, the two of them linked: the spiritual love is extended from God to man and then reflected by man, who is made in the image of God, back to God. God gives man the power to act as God acts, since God is love: man then reflects God's power in his own human actions towards others.

You might think it an odd thing to say when talking about charity, but I try not to lend things to people, because the act of lending is fraught with trouble: the lender expects the item back but the lendee may forget to return it, which itself causes tension. It's for this very reason that I don't often lend books. Instead, I give them to people with no expectation of return: that way, it's a gift from me to them, and the parameters of the transaction are much more defined and less complex. Besides, giving a book is itself an act of love. To think of what someone would really like or need, to share with them something you yourself have really liked – this is charity in its medieval form right here, the display of love for someone else through the donation of what has moved you at a spiritual level. Finding someone who loves books which you love is a great thing.

I like to think well of people – I believe that most people are fundamentally good and decent, though I'm aware that many others think this a hopelessly naïve point of view, and I must admit there are times when the rather Panglossian benevolence of my outlook is sorely tested – but when it comes to absolutely unconditional love, few things beat my horses. I've got far too many of them, but each has a shared history. A couple are rescue cases, some semi-retired, one is stone deaf, one blind in one eye and I happily spend vast amounts of time with them and on them – two hours every morning before my other work, two hours again in the evening when I've finished, and then both days at the weekend, at least five hours a day or more in the long summer season. I'm actually in the saddle for well over twenty hours a week, sometimes training with weapons like sword, axe and lance, other times working on a young horse and training it to perform, or even hacking out across the landscape on mini adventures. That's as much time as some of my fellow re-enactors get to ride every year. So I'm probably riding as much, or perhaps even more than, a medieval knight would have done back in the day.

I switch off by talking to my horses. Yes, seriously. After a long day at work there's nothing I love more than going for a ride in the countryside. I offload by chatting to my horse. It also puts my brain into neutral and helps me process things. I could watch (and indeed have watched) horses for hundreds of hours. They communicate with each other by movements so subtle that the untrained human eye can easily miss them: their posture, their approach, the way they hold and move their ears, nostrils or eyes. I can look at someone riding a horse and see whether the horse is paying attention to the rider or to something else, or occasionally to both as the ears can be independently targeted. Horses to me are easily as fascinating as humans, perhaps even more so, and attempt to communicate with us much more than most people think.

Horses vary hugely in price. I have some which have cost £25,000 or more to buy, while others are rescues which cost me nothing. (In medieval times, a very good warhorse could be worth the equivalent of £250,000 today.) But the big cost of horses is keeping them. Every horse will probably cost up to, and sometimes beyond, a hundred quid a week to look after: food, bedding, vets' bills, getting hay cut from the fields and so on. Horses are money pits, but they're lovely money pits. And a massive time sink too. Even so, I could afford to get staff to do it all for me, but that would negate the whole point of me having them. I do all their training myself. It's hard work – I don't need to go to the gym because I'm literally trundling wheelbarrows filled with shit every day of my life – but I seldom think of it as a chore. I love doing it.

Horses are my friends, part of my family, and they have been for as long as I can remember. I managed to persuade my parents to give up foreign holidays and instead buy me a pony when I was eight years old, and have never looked back. I was one of the few boys who went to Pony Club, and I won Best Boy two years in a row. (The fact that I was competing in a field of three, rather than several dozen girls, was of course only a minor detail.) And I used to love Australian author Elyne Mitchell's *Silver Brumby* series. There were six or seven books (she wrote a few more in the 1990s, by which time I was involved with Rebellion) set in the Snowy Mountains region of Australia and detailing the adventures of Thowra, a magnificent pale brumby (Australian wild horse) stallion and his descendants.

Here the horses were the heroes and mankind the villains: Thowra's cream coat and silvery mane meant he was a prized target for hunters, and his mother Bel Bel had taught him all she knew of the high country and the dangers of man alike. Mitchell's worldbuilding was the equal of any of those mentioned in the previous chapter: I found myself carried away by the richness of this environment and the trials and tribulations of Thowra and his friends and rivals. Thowra's very name, the Aboriginal word for 'wind', spoke of both his wild untamed nature (he was born in a storm) and the threat which would always hang over him, as he would have to be as fast as the wind to remain free. He needed to be cunning and brave, not just in relation to humans but other stallions too who were jealous of his unusual appearance (most brumbies being black, bay, brown and grey).

This love of horses was part of a wider childhood passion for wildlife and landscapes. One of my earliest memories is finding a frog in the garden and literally jumping for joy. I'd always be building dens with whatever came to hand: fallen branches, dead leaves, pieces of moss. Sometimes at school

I'd see my friends treating animals as playthings – messing around with them at best, being actively cruel at worst – and I always felt that their behaviour was weird and disturbing in a very deep and primal way. I was too young to know the exact ramifications of it, or that cruelty to animals is one third of the homicidal triad which is exhibited in part or whole by many adult murderers (arson and bedwetting being the other two): I just knew that someone who was happy to pull the wings off flies or belt frogs in the air with tennis rackets was someone I needed to fundamentally re-evaluate, both as a person and in terms of my friendship with them.

My choice was at one stage to go to university or become a professional showjumper, but the latter was way too expensive. I did think about being a vet and spent a week travelling with one, but the fact that so much of his time was spent necessarily putting animals to sleep really distressed me. It wasn't the way he did it – he was very compassionate and caring – but the simple fact he had to do it at all, and so often as well. I knew that the only way to get used to it would be to inure myself to it through willpower and/or practice, and I didn't really want to become numb to or blasé about animal suffering. Sometimes we were called out because someone had died and their surviving partner wanted the animals put down, which staggered me. He gave no external hints that any of this affected him, which I guess was one of the ways in which he could do his job. (He was also nicknamed the Pink Panther as his hands were always stained with pink antiseptic fluid.)

There have been a handful of years when I haven't had a horse in my life, but only a handful. Picking out a favourite of the ones I have now is impossible as so many have been so important to me, but sadly they age at a much faster rate than we do, so horse relationships must, by necessity come and go.

I'll mention some of my most memorable early horses and ponies here, but all of them have been important. My first pony was the ironically nomenclatured Mr. Snuff, who was apparently named for his colour which was a speckled brown, but might have more properly been named after a master assassin. I think he was potentially one of the most devious and lethal creatures I've ever ridden, but it taught me how to land on the ground and get back on again and he wasn't very accurate with his bites or kicks and occasionally tried to avoid stamping on you. Following him was the angelic Smokey Joe, or more formally Silver Arrow, a beautiful grey (so white to most people) Welsh pony. Most recently if I had to pick one it would be Warlord, who appears in a lot of my YouTube videos. Warlord is a Lusitano who was gelded very late, so he behaves a bit like a stallion but lacks the muscular neck. (Gelding is castrating stallions (male horses) to make them less likely to get distracted by their hormones, and has been practised over the past two millennia by many equestrian cultures, though not all: for example, Arab cultures tended to keep stallions in bachelor herds while mares were used for riding, so they didn't geld much.) Stallions, geldings and mares (female horses) are all wonderful to work with. I find stallions can be impulsive and mares can be changeable, whereas geldings are pretty stable overall usually.

Medieval knights in Western Europe would probably have ridden stallions to war, if the pictorial evidence is to be believed. Mostly because a stallion's musculature is more developed than that of a mare or gelding, and there's something in the fightyness of some stallions that makes them want to go into battle. Medieval styles of riding were different from what we're used to today. The saddles were designed to keep the rider's body upright and their legs long, with high fronts and backs, so jumping obstacles (which is easier if the rider can flex their legs and get up and out of the saddle with the movement) isn't that easy. There was probably an emphasis on what in equestrian circles is called collection. This is where the horse seems to gather itself up under the rider, perhaps carrying more weight on its hind legs than its front ones. This makes manoeuvring more rapid and helps the horse biomechanically carry the rider's weight better so it not only makes for a more controlled and controllable steed but is also easiest for the horse. In some ways it's a bit like a tennis player standing ready to receive a serve, tensed and ready to reach in the direction needed. Medieval horses needed explosive power to accelerate towards a target, or change direction in an instant, but they also needed to be able to remain calm in incredibly stressful situations. Imagine the chaos of a battlefield with sound and fury everywhere: the clanging of weapons on armour, the screams of injured and dying men and animals, the stench of blood and faeces from men and horses, great heraldic banners snapping in the wind, trumpets and drums, the occasional bark of an early medieval hand cannon, and movement every which way as animals and men alike surge and recoil. Horses are not evolved to deal with that, so the training needed to have an effective weapon platform made of flesh and blood would be extensive, hence the great cost of a destrier.

I've been using horses for medieval recreation for the past fifteen years or so, with my first generation of self-bred warhorses. Before that I was playing polo for five years. Then I felt I had to explore this forgotten area of equestrian skill. The horse and knight were almost synonymous. If you look at dressage today, much of the discipline has come (via a roundabout route, of course) from medieval knightly riding: dressage is basically the art of horse manoeuvring for practical purposes. Even though the kind of reconstructions and recreations I do can't be nearly as visceral and terrifying as the real thing, there's still quite enough going on for me to need to train my horses patiently and specifically for such situations. A horse is unlikely to understand that a re-enactment battlefield is not a lethal place to be.

A horse's natural instinct, and best chance of survival in the wild, is to run away from danger, unfamiliar smells and discordant sounds. Kicking and biting are a last resort, but if in doubt run away as fast as you can (probably something that should be taught in self-defence classes as a priority). Millions of years of evolution have honed its instincts to run away fast, and keep running until you can run no more. Horses are very good at running and find comfort in motion. Many in the field will simply run with their friends for fun, tails up and the horse equivalent of big grins on their faces. Most horses find standing still when anxious to be almost impossible; even walking them in small circles makes them feel like they're doing the right thing and moving away from danger: therefore any horse must be trained not to do what it instinctively wants to do when confronted by a threat. When training my horses, not to actual battle, but to simulated battle and even the hustle and bustle of a film set, I get them used to those smells and sounds little by little, praising when they get things right and trying again when it doesn't work (no physical punishment ever). We also put dead bodies (simulated, obviously) into the mix. A hay-stuffed boiler suit makes a convincing enough battlefield casualty. Trial and error is a big part of this kind of training: progress is rarely linear, and what can feel like a real advance one day is incredibly frustrating the next. Being patient with a horse when it's learning is an activity. Often they will need time to come to terms with a new thing that is worrying them.

Rushing a training session is a bad thing to do as it sets up negative associations. If you're feeling angry or upset yourself it's best not to try to train a horse, just go for a ride and relax. I think it's likely a horse can smell your stress and probably hear your heart beating wildly.

You have to work with your horse. It sounds obvious, but to maximise the potential of what you can do on horseback you have to almost think of yourself as one entity: not rider and horse but rider-and-horse, a mythical hybrid beast, a centaur. Reins, bridle, legs and weight are not mere straps and buckles: they're all conduits for your synapses and nerves to join seamlessly with theirs. They're communications links along which you can have a discussion with another living breathing creature. A skilled rider, for example, can use their own bodyweight to move the horse sideways without either looking at them or speaking, and for a knight sideways movement was critical: it allowed him to keep facing the enemy while simultaneously keeping his options open. A surprisingly large number of modern people simply don't know that a horse can move sideways rather than just forward and backwards. It's something that medieval people would have known fully, but these days, sadly, so few people get the chance to spend any significant time with large animals like horses.

And of course the hybrid beast of rider and horse is much more imposing than either of them on their own. A rearing and plunging horse threatens the foot soldiers around it which in turn makes space and allows it to get out of danger: a knight seated on top of a horse has a huge advantage of height and reach not just at close quarters but also in terms of being able to see what's going on over a wide area. A static horse is more vulnerable than a rapidly moving one which is one of the biggest things movies get wrong about cavalry. Do not stay still if you are fighting from atop a horse. Use the horse's speed and movement to get into and out of the combat. A riding horse is likely at least 400 kilos in weight, probably much more, so any physical collision with a puny foot soldier is likely to smash them out of the way with ease. Horses can be very intimidating if you don't know them and you don't see them often, which if you live in a city you may well not do. Their power and size are awe-inspiring. When Hernan Cortes landed in what is now Mexico to conquer the Aztec Empire in 1519, it was the first time any of the locals had seen a horse, and to them the horses must have seemed like literal mythical beasts as if someone turned up to a fight with an actual dragon. Cortes galloped the horses up and down the beach to the accompaniment of cannon fire, a display of power and might which would be like an alien civilisation landing in our world with weaponry so advanced we hadn't even conceived of the possibility of its existence.

Of course, all the horse and armour stuff, whilst fully authentic and genuinely a big part of my everyday life, also has value for public relations. Many journalists who come to interview me want images to go with the story, preferably visually interesting ones. Images that will catch the putative reader's eye. A picture of me dressed as a knight, even if the article is about some technical corner of the games industry and therefore of no direct relevance, is all of the above. There have been numerous occasions when I've been asked to be novelty-photographed sitting at my desk in armour, something I've not yet agreed to actually do. I think it'd look pretty silly. Sometimes saying, 'No, I don't think that's a good idea,' is what being a leader means, and sometimes it stops you looking like a prat. The publicity angle is absolutely not why I do it. If it was just about the publicity there'd be easier ways, and cheaper ones, and certainly ones that don't involve so many wheelbarrows full of dung.

At a very basic level, horses are the exact counterpoint to the rest of my life. Computer games are by definition hi-tech: we might not be right on the edge of computing technology, but we're not far off it, at least not in areas such as graphics capability. Horses are very low tech, arguably some of the lowest around. The vast, vast majority of what I do with them is the same as riders were doing 100 years ago, 200 years ago, 500 years ago, 1,000 years ago. I even have a training manual for chariot ponies written by Kikkuli in the Hittite language some 3,500 years ago (mine's a translation, I don't read or write ancient Hittite, just to be clear). It's pretty good stuff too, if a little harsh in places, and sets out a daily training regimen that will get chariot ponies fit for battle in a few months. I've been tempted to try it, but it's hard work for the trainer too. Fifty years ago, mass-market personal computers didn't even exist: yet equestrian technology, if you can call it that, has hardly moved on in ten times that amount of time. I still recognise horse equipment that's on display in museums, and have things like it in my tack room in regular use, just made of slightly different materials like stainless steel rather than bronze. I'd like to think that ancient Hittite pony trainers would be right at home on my yard. We'd probably share tips.

It's not because people have forgotten about horses: quite the opposite. It's that the basics have worked perfectly for so long that there's no need to reinvent the wheel for the sake of it. Whether the wheel or the domestication of horses came first is up for discussion. This wider question of technology and what it represents in social, psychological and emotional terms is discussed more fully in Chapter Eleven, 'Hope', but my equestrian interest has shown me the importance of sticking with what works rather than just assuming that something new will be better. Sales people are always trying to tell you that new is better, and sometimes it is, but not always; sometimes change is bad.

Of course, there's always room for overlap between old and new, between ancient and modern. I enjoy games about medieval fantasy warfare, such as *Kingdom Come: Deliverance* and *Mount & Blade: Warband*, but I haven't played either for long as I've been just too busy with the real thing. We did make a game called *Joust Legend*, a mobile game about medieval tournaments in which the player takes on the role of a knight and participates in jousting matches. (I discuss jousting in Chapter Twelve, 'Valour'.)

What do games usually get wrong about horses? Almost everything, but especially movement. Anybody who rides to a certain level knows about collection (which we've already discussed), transitions (changing gaits, from a walk to a trot, a trot to a canter, and a canter to a gallop) and lateral work (any movement other than straight forward). So in order to make it as realistic as possible, we used motion capture on a horse and rider – yes, you guessed it, Warlord and me. Doing motion capture is quite an odd experience. Both Warlord and I had to be encased in Lycra with reflective dots at certain places, which made him look black (he's normally white) and also made me worry about overheating (him and me both). The Lycra was quite slippery against the saddle, so that wasn't much fun either. And, since Warlord tends to get worked up the longer the shoot goes on, we did the slow stuff first before going for the more active crazy stuff at the end. One of our senior staff tells a funny story about pulling a buttock muscle badly when trying to lurch out of our way during one run. Well I did warn them beforehand that we'd be going quite quickly.

But it all proved worth it, because I think the game really has an authenticity of movement which couldn't be found any other way. We've all seen actors pretend riding horses, and anybody who knows anything about riding can instantly tell they're not actually on a horse at all, but some mechanical rig that goes up and down at the wrong speed (why can't they get that right I always ask, and it's probably because the director themselves doesn't recognise the error or it'd be fixed asap). Also actors sometimes exaggerate their expertise to get a job. I was on one film set with an actor who shall remain nameless. We were both on horses. I was beside him when I noticed a certain level of stress on his face. I gently asked if there was anything I could do to help, thinking that something might be wrong with his horse, and he told me he was terrified as we had to canter up a hill to the top and he'd exaggerated his abilities to get the job. It turns out he'd more than exaggerated, he'd outright lied. We worked out that I'd ride alongside him and grab his reins to take control if needed. It all worked out in the end. The trouble is being on a horse and being out of control can be very dangerous indeed, both to cast and crew and most importantly the other horses.

Back to horses and movement; even in games, part of the issue is that animators look for references in the wrong places without realising that there are differences between areas and styles. I've lost count of the number of times I've had to nudge an animator to ignore the wrong style of horse riding. For example, they may reference western loping in a game of high school dressage. If you don't know horses, it's all just horses, but there are huge differences in the different disciplines of various areas of equestrianism. So seeing Warlord's movement on a computer generated horse was a lot of fun but also a sign of authenticity. You can recognise both him and me in the game easily, or at least I can. I enjoyed doing the game, though it wasn't our biggest commercial success (not that I expected it to be): it was niche and experimental, which is something we pride ourselves on doing sometimes, and it was a good learning curve (especially technically) and taught us some things to do going forward. Past and future in harmony, which is always a good thing to see.

Chapter Three

Justice

THE QUEST FOR and maintenance of justice was one of the most important roles a medieval knight had, and I regard it as a non-negotiable in anyone who considers themself a decent person. In his treatise on knighthood and chivalry, the 13th-century knight Ramon Lull spoke of the importance of the knight's coat. 'A coat is given to a knight in significance of the great hardships that a knight must suffer to honour chivalry, for likewise as the coat is above the other garments of iron, and is in the rain and receives the strokes before the hauberk and other armours, right so is a knight chosen to sustain greater travaille than a lesser man. And all the men who are under his nobility, and in his guard ought to be when they have need to have recourse to him. And the knight ought to defend them after his power. And the knights ought rather to be taken, hurt or dead, than this happen to the men under their guard. Then as it is right and great chivalry, therefore the princes and barons in such great travaille to keep their lands and people.'

This is, I feel, the crux of justice: to always don the coat which allows you to endure not so much physical as emotional discomfort. It's not just a case of the knight defending those who depend on him, and therefore some form of *noblesse oblige*: it's the responsibility of us all to risk mockery and disdain in order to make a stand on something that's right, no matter how unpopular that stand may be. It's easier to walk on by if you see someone being bullied or harassed, if you hear someone being offensive: easier to act like the three monkeys and pretend that if you didn't see it or hear it then you don't have to speak about it.

In Chartres Cathedral, a knightly prayer carved in stone reads in part: 'Most Holy Lord, Almighty Father... thou who hast permitted on earth the use of the sword to repress the malice [evil] of the wicked and defend justice... cause thy servant here before thee, by disposing [turning] his heart to goodness, never to use this sword or another to injure anyone unjustly; but let him use it always to defend the just and right.'

The sword is of course traditionally associated with justice, not just in knightly terms but more general ones too. The statue of Lady Justice above London's Old Bailey (the Central Criminal Court of England and Wales), for example, holds a sword in her right hand and a pair of scales in her left (a pairing common to many statues of Lady Justice throughout the world). The sword represents authority (often in the olden days with the implicit understanding that it could be used to administer the death penalty), and the scales the competing claims of each side and the need to weigh them impartially. The sword of justice can be a terrible thing, so it must be tempered by humanity and mercy. You might be interested to know that there were specific execution swords made for that particular awful purpose, often without a stabbing point and quite tip heavy compared to a blade built for battle.

Justice is action to ensure that all members of society receive fair treatment. Justice is not just a morally correct course to pursue but also a sensible one in terms of overall group satisfaction and cohesion. An organisation which is seen to be run on fair lines both by those inside and outside will be more productive and stable, certainly in the medium to long term, than one where senior executives play favourites, where workplace procedures are skewed, and so on. That kind of disruptive, lopsided culture may be successful in the short term, where people are energized by fear for their jobs, but it will also lead to high staff turnover and structural instability. Justice, of course, is quite distinct from what is legal. What is strictly legal and following the letter of the law may not be justice at all and, in some circumstances, justice can only be achieved by breaking the law.

There are supposedly four main types of justice, and I try to pay each of them mind when the need for them occurs in business or life:

- *distributive justice,* which ensures that everybody gets their fair share. The issue here, of course, is what counts as a 'fair share' and who decides that. In an ideal company people should be paid appropriately to the circumstances, including their skill and experience. This doesn't mean that everyone gets the same; far from it. Some people have more responsibility than others: some people are more skilled or have more experience than others, even those ostensibly at the same rank or with the same job title (I'm not big on strict vertical hierarchy or rigid job titles anyway). People should feel they get a fair crack of the whip and that their efforts are appreciated both financially and in more general terms too, and notice I have deliberately avoided using the term human resources. I dislike that term, though it has its uses. Resources are electricity, computers, desks, toilet paper, raw materials, all the non-human things that go to make an organisation. People are not in the same category, they are the life blood of any company.

- *procedural justice*, which ensures that people receive fair treatment in issues such as disputes and appraisals. This means there must be rules which are not simply 'fair' but also widely considered to be fair (hence receiving 'buy-in' from everyone concerned) and applied impartially. The most equitable rulebook is useless if it's applied selectively: any law is only ever as good as its enforcement. Those charged with overseeing the process must also be seen as neutral and unbiased. Clearly in any dispute the eventual decision is almost certainly going to disappoint and dissatisfy at least one party (and maybe both), but they are more likely to accept it if they have also accepted the rationale and procedures that have led to that decision.

- *retributive justice* means punishment for an offence or wrongdoing, and *restorative justice* seeks ways to make amends for those offences both on individual and social levels. Clearly as a business owner I have much less to do with these types than I do with the first two. Of course we have systems in place for work transgressions, and available sanctions go all the way up from an informal warning to dismissal, but to be honest once things have got to that point with an employee then the system has probably failed in one way or another anyway. If I get distributive and procedural justices right, I should by definition obviate the need for retributive and restorative justices. I'm running a computer games company, not the prison system. It is, I guess, a sort of deterrent, but not in conventional terms. The usual idea behind deterrence is that the punishment for committing a crime outweighs any possible gains from that crime, but here it's more that the entire system – if I've got it right – mitigates against people wanting to step outside it in the first place.

In the next chapter, 'Sagacity', I talk more about negotiations and ensuring that both sides are mostly happy with a deal. It's a sensible thing to do for several business-related reasons, particularly in terms of fostering long-term relationships, but more than that it's the *right* thing to do. A commitment to justice involves a commitment to doing the right thing, morally, at all times, not just when it suits you or when it coincides with other less altruistic motivations. If you're not committed to justice even – especially – when it may cost you in other ways, you're not really committed to it at all. I have on occasion negotiated myself down as the other side would not have been able to uphold their side of the bargain with the deal they were offering: it was too cheap, and if we'd agreed that super cheap price, it would have caused problems for us both in the future. In one case they were confused, in the other obviously very grateful; both deals worked out well for us all in the end.

I try to seek always the path of 'right', unencumbered by bias or personal interest as much as possible, and remember to be chivalric. When one is striving to do the right thing, as with everyone, this is easier said than done given how easily we can convince ourselves that our own interests converge with a more objective concept of the good path. Being just involves being honest and fair. But honesty doesn't mean telling everyone your secrets, and fairness doesn't mean being weak and letting other people walk all over you. You can be honest while keeping information to yourself, and indeed you'd be a fool not to do so, but there's a big difference between that and outright lying. I don't lie in business. If I don't want to answer a question I'll say so, but I don't tell flat-out lies. I once amused a well-known BBC journalist who asked me an over-zealous question. I said, politely, I was not going to answer it. Fairness by definition can't mean letting someone else walk all over you, as that would be no more fair than them letting me do the same to them.

Justice has to apply across all areas of life. You have to do the right thing even when nobody's watching, or else it's just selective expediency. (Maybe that's where religion comes in a little bit: trying to convince people there's someone or something watching.) In my opinion, victory or success has no meaning unless it's been won fairly. If I'm jousting and someone's got a problem, a horse is not running safely, or a visor is unfastened, I just pull my lance up and don't hit them. I could hit them and score points, and have been criticised for doing what I do, as apparently I lack the urge to win, but winning at all costs is not the aim, especially if it isn't right to do so. Fight hard, try to win, but also realise that loss can be as valuable and as much a learning experience as gain; just make sure you get up again and keep on going. Once I was given some inside information from somebody about a business competitor who was in a bad way financially and there was an opportunity for me to take advantage of that. I felt it was inappropriate, especially as someone had tipped me off about them, so I ignored the opportunity even though it would've probably made us a lot of money. There was a clear chance to unfairly take advantage of somebody's ill fortune, which I turned down on principle.

I've probably been offered bribes in the past, not explicitly as such, but by implication, and have not so much refused outright as not even been aware that I've been offered them until someone else has pointed it out later. This must have been totally infuriating for the person doing the offering – clearly people aren't totally direct about these kinds of approaches: they tend to couch it in the language of 'gifts', 'rewards', 'sweeteners', 'mutual benefits', 'favours' and so on – but on the flipside, my obtuseness in these matters is probably not a bad reputation to have. If people know that's your reputation then they're less likely to try it on.

I try to lift up everyone in my industry. As mentioned before, I co-founded and chaired the video game trade association, TIGA. Every single other organisation that was a founding member, including one that joined later but stroppily insisted they be called a founding member, have all either gone bust or been bought and dissolved into other organisations. Rebellion is the last survivor, like the lone gladiator in a Roman arena, surrounded by the dead. In 2014 my brother and I came up with the idea of a tax break for game developers and, along with TIGA and other peers and supporters in the industry, overcame many obstacles over several years to get it approved by the UK government. Several of our colleagues and one trade body actively campaigned against it, which was a bit of a weird thing, but they're on-board now of course. This is the Video Games Tax Relief, which currently allows British developers to reclaim about twenty percent of production costs if their game passes a cultural test such as having a British character or setting. It's a lot more complex than that of course, and forms need to be filled in, audits made, but it's a decent chunk of money or equity back to the developer. The impact has been dramatic: many hundreds of millions of pounds have been paid out in relief since the initial introduction, and there has been an ongoing and steady increase in the number of jobs in the industry and an improved amount of inward investment. I'd seen how Canada had used tax incentives to build a thriving computer games industry more or less from scratch, and I wanted the same kind of central support for the UK industry. The UK industry was being slowly etched away by other places in the world and we were gracefully slipping down the global pecking order. My logic, which I argued vociferously to the government, is that the games industry is a sector which produces highly skilled, intelligent and creative workers, and which sells a product that is in high demand all around the world: in other words, exactly the sort of industry the government should be supporting, and indeed exactly the kind of industry it does already support (film, STEM-based R&D, and so on). These industries rely on the movement of talented people around the world and the exchange of ideas and skills, all of which help keep a country's economy vibrant and progressive. I had to help guide the legislation too, helping civil servants understand what's involved in making a game and therefore making sure they're always fit for purpose. One of my favourite observations which I subsequently heard repeated back to me was that the government needed to construct a tax incentive that was like a wide gate but not a missing fence.

I also try to keep a sense of fairness about the games we make and how we make them. We make games we want to play, because that way we know we're doing them for the right reasons. We're not trying to make games that pretend to be movies, as some people like to do. We're not trying to make gougey gambling mechanisms to grab money off people. We're trying to make games we want to play and that others will too. Ideally I want a lot of people to buy our games, play them, enjoy them, think they're worth the money, put them down and go and do something else. And I'm fine with that. That's all we need to be successful, and if people like one of our games it makes them more likely to buy another, hopefully creating a virtuous cycle and a lot of repeated business for us.

And quite frankly I only want to do stuff that I can be enthusiastic about, be proud we've made, and happy that people are playing it. I find it slightly creepy when I talk to some other developers and find out that they have behavioural psychologists working for them, using a lot of psychological tricks which they've imported from the gambling industry. Somehow that feels wrong and unfair to me. I suppose there can be a fine line between persuading someone to buy your game and tricking them into paying for it, but I think it's a pretty brightly coloured fine line. In some business models a game maker might only get one percent of players to pay them any money at all, but one percent of a lot of players is still a healthy revenue stream, so the aim is to get as many people playing as possible and therefore increase the value of that one percent. There's big business there, and a lot of people are very happy working in it. It's very scientific, analytical and highly skilled. Small percentage differences in human behaviour can multiply up to large sums of actual money. My ideal game depends heavily on that nebulous concept that is good gameplay. When I'm studying and developing gameplay, I'm looking at trying to entertain people and help them escape from their daily woes, stresses and strains for a moment. I don't want to just distract them for thirty seconds while they're waiting for a bus. Ideally I want them to be engrossed in and consumed by a new world that is unlike our 'real' one. I want the player to feel empowered but challenged and thrilled. I want them to explore and discover and remember what they're doing, and maybe carry some of those memorable moments with them when they're not holding a controller or sitting at a keyboard. You can probably tell I'm particularly interested in the fully immersive experience that a good game can bring.

There's always a balance to be struck between rights and responsibilities. I believe very strongly that businesses should pay their social dues. This isn't just tax, though obviously that's a large part of it: it's holiday pay, sickness pay, national insurance contributions and so on, as well as helping people into entry-level jobs and having school students spend a few days in a professional work environment. These are all costs to a company in the short term, but a net gain in the long term for everybody. It boils my blood when I see companies exploit the gig economy – I won't name names, but I'm sure you can guess the kind of outfits I'm talking about – moving heaven and earth to classify their workers as contractors rather than employees so they don't have to be responsible for those kinds of costs. These are the normal margins which businesses have to deal with, and to somehow try and duck them is wrong both in the short term and long term. Legislation will catch up with these companies over time, and whatever their share price now, buoyed by not paying their social dues, there will be a financial reckoning and a social one too. It's likely that some people will make a ton of money quickly and some will lose it when the tide turns. As a company owner you should feel a sense of genuine responsibility towards your employees rather than treating them as a cost drain. Again, there's a big gap between what's immoral and what's illegal. If the legality of something is your only criterion for deciding its morality, then you're copping out of the kind of decisions any responsible adult should be making. At the risk of taking things to a dark place, we all know of historical situations in the 20th century where literal atrocities have been technically legal at the time. The 19th century railroad tycoon James Hill had a similar view of collective responsibility. Externally, he called out his rivals for seeking subsidies, hiking rates, manipulating stock and not running their railroads for long-term gain: internally, he wouldn't ask his workmen to do anything he wouldn't do, which included the time his train was caught in a blizzard and he personally wielded a shovel in six feet of snow to help dig the train out.

Technology has also brought about questions of copyright and the exploitation of intellectual property. YouTube and other early online digital video platforms grew, at least in part, during a time when using copyright material without explicit permission was a bit of a wild west frontier. It has been argued that parts of its business model implicitly depended on the owners of those copyrights either being unaware of the situation, slow to protect their rights or not doing so at all. Creators on YouTube were able to take advantage of unclear rules, complex enforcement procedures and of the inadequacy of legislation in an area moving way faster than lawmakers' responses (and covering many jurisdictions too, further proving the inadequacies of national laws when dealing with transnational entities). Oh, people say, it's just videos, no one's getting harmed (you see this still with bullshit disclaimers on posted videos saying, 'No copyright infringement intended', when the infringement is literally taking place before your eyes).

There is a discussion to be had about fair use and the ability to build on other creatives' work of course, and review and criticism, but just taking someone else's work and reposting it without permission seems to be clearly wrong. To be fair to YouTube they have changed their rules significantly since those early days and try hard to balance competing perspectives on rights and their uses.

However you see the protection of other people's creative efforts, copyright exists for a reason: to ensure that the people whose talent and hard work has created something in the first place can benefit from its success, and ultimately make more. With a set duration on copyright, eventually such works will enter the public domain to the benefit of us all, but in the interim the owners will have had a decent crack at making money from it. That seems to me to be a fair solution in principle, though arguments about how long such protection should last continue to rage, and such oddities as music having less time protection than written works do seem odd to me.

The rules around copyright, and the very name of the time-limited state-granted monopoly, came from the rise in printing technology and the right of book makers to prevent others simply making copies and selling them without any of the investment. There was a time, obviously, when there was no law against making copies of books, and the legislation had to catch up with the rapidly moving change in the media, which should sound very familiar to you. An interesting area for modern day right holders is the rise in people making fan works. Amateur productions that come from an affection for the source material. That's why we have strict rules when dealing with content creators who, for example, want to make fan short videos involving *2000 AD* characters, or create fan art based on our characters. The easiest and simplest way would be to bring out the ban hammer hard and just forbid it and say no, ultimately getting lawyers to write letters and issuing what are known as take-down notices to get content removed. Many rights holders of big brands do exactly this. Our considered opinion currently is that would not only be excessively draconian but also an abject failure to recognise that most people who make this kind of content do so from love for the source material and a positive passion to get involved somehow. So we tend to allow it on two conditions: that it's not done for profit, and that there's no crowdsourcing and raising money to do it via public platforms. You want to do it off your own bat, purely for your own pleasure and with your own money (or money raised privately from family and friends)? Knock yourself out, and let us know beforehand (and afterwards). If it's good enough we'll let other fans know about your work. But otherwise, no.

This question of rights and responsibilities was one which also vexed our ancestors. Many would-be knights in the late Middle Ages refused knighthood because of the higher tax rates they would have to pay, and the greater expenses for war equipment and social responsibilities that came with it. A knight was expected to be able to live up to a standard. There was a measure of land, which was quite variable in acreage (as it depends on the quality of the land), but was of between 300 to 1,000 acres, called, appropriately enough, a Knight's Fee. This increased financial burden of becoming a knight meant that laws were introduced to literally force squires to become knights even against their will. (A similar phenomenon, though thankfully without the threat of legal enforcement, can be seen amongst barristers, where some practitioners don't attempt to take silk (become a QC) even though they'd have a good chance of being appointed, because they fear that, since a QC's fees are much higher than those of a junior (non-QC), they'd lose work in the short to medium term, perhaps to a catastrophic degree. And since all non-QC barristers are called juniors, it's therefore very common for even those close to retirement age to still be technically a junior. (One way of feeling younger than you are, I suppose.)

Medieval justice could be high, middle or low, depending on the severity of the offence and the maximum possible punishment. Knights were most often involved in low justice for minor offences, as middle justice involved full civil and criminal jurisdiction and high justice involved capital crimes and the right to inflict corporal punishment, torture and even the death penalty (the authorities holding these rights were said to have *ius gladii*, the 'right of the sword', which again taps into the trope of a sword being an instrument of justice rather than simply a neutral weapon).

Of course, the nature and severity of crimes varies over time and according to the social conditions and mores of the time. We can laugh at how seriously medieval justice treated offences like pig stealing, tree felling and field ploughing, but in an almost totally agrarian culture these were hugely and fundamentally important. Stealing a man's livestock or wood wasn't a prank or a minor misdemeanour: it was a grave threat to his livelihood and well-being. A more recent representation of this might be the capital punishment meted out for horse thieves in the Old West. The impact of the crime being reflected in the severity of the punishment.

Justice was also tied into one's status in society, as indeed it still is today. The king would often travel the country staying with noblemen and knights, and though this was a great honour, it was also a great (and very costly) burden – the king came with an entourage which even a modern-day pop megastar might balk at, and that entourage didn't stint on their consumption of food and drink. Some knights and noblemen would even claim that the plague had come to dissuade the king from turning up and eating them out of house and home. But these visits (assuming that the monarch had seen through the plague excuse) were also a reflection of how knighthood was changing: having started as a catch-all term for brutal soldiers, the concept had gradually become refined to the point of rewarding people for their contributions to society and tasking them with the administration of justice. Today's judicial system has evolved greatly from those days, but the concept of knighthood as reward still very much exists, though of course today's knights are no longer required to fight battles on horseback, nor indeed to show much by way of chivalric virtue. Personally I think they should at least be able to ride a horse and handle a lance and sword, if only for the sake of tradition, but I suppose that would limit the numbers far too severely these days.

The way our society is set up mitigates against justice, however. The networks in which we live our lives – social networks, political networks, financial networks – are, some would say, set up for psychopaths to succeed. It's one of those wetware bugs in human psychology: it's human nature to be attracted to people with psychopathic qualities, even though they tend to do terrible jobs of managing things to genuine widespread social benefit. If you think about it, who'd want to be a politician? It's in many ways a shitty job. You work insanely long hours, you spend a lot of time apart from your family, you have to deal with toxic party politics day in day out, you're not especially well paid given the demands of the job, and at any given time a substantial proportion of the population think you're not just wrong but actively evil and therefore hate you at a visceral level. It's a job which seems to attract a limited number of people. This is manifestly not a good thing for society. Two things might help our political classes; if they used evidence and followed the data rather than party dogma, and if they were obliged to swear to uphold the Chivalric Code alongside the oath to the monarch. If that happened the world would be a better place and a more noble one.

Chapter Four

Sagacity

SAGACITY IS THE twin capacity to understand and assess: to see the truth of a situation and to know how best to use that to one's own advantage. Both parts are equally important. To mix metaphors, there's not much mileage in being smart enough to drill down into the nuts and bolts of, say, a deal unless you put that wisdom to some practical application, be it on your own terms or in advising someone else. Conversely, unless you do understand properly, your judgment will always run the risk of being wrong more often than necessary: maybe not on this deal or even the next one, but sooner or later you'll come unstuck.

Sagacity is of course a prerequisite in so many aspects of business. Some of them are covered in other chapters (dealing with people in Chapter Eight, 'Truth'; making a good computer game in Chapter Ten, 'Diligence'; seeking out new markets in

Chapter Twelve, 'Valour'), so here I'll concentrate on three areas: negotiation, data and behaviour.

Negotiation. The best business is always done by helping other people achieve their aims too, so that you reach a position of mutual benefit. If every deal is screwing over the other person, what does that say about you? People are obsessed with the ridiculously foolish idea that every deal has to have a winner and a loser, and that rather like the old adage that there's a sucker at every poker table and if you can't work out who the sucker is then it has to be you, if you don't know that you're the winner then you must be the loser. This seems to be the basis of a lot of short-term, make-it-quick business thinking where doing actual business is not the aim, but the manner in which you try to make loads of money, fast. I call it the soufflé method of business, cook it quick whilst it's filled with air and take it out of the oven at the right time. In cooking, soufflés often end up as quiches.

But why should it be that way? Why does every deal have to be a zero sum? Obviously, in life as in business, it doesn't. Clearly it's a rare situation in which interests converge so perfectly and terms mesh like perfectly machined cogs in a device so that everyone gets exactly what they want, but there's usually significant areas of reasonable common ground in the middle where no-one has had to compromise too far on something fundamental to them, and where everyone can come away with enough of what they'd wanted to feel that the deal is a fair one while also recognising that the other side has had to give up some of their wish list too. When somebody does you a disservice there's a fair chance that you'll try to seek to redress the balance later on, so the same is true the other way round. Most people, but not all, like to return good behaviour with good behaviour if they can. Humans are social creatures and have evolved to cooperate.

I like to think that people who have done good business with me once will do business with me again. An ultra-aggressive approach to business can help you win in the short term, depending on the nature of the power dynamic between you and them, but in the long term you burn bridges and eventually only the desperate will do deals with you as they have no option. People won't be doing you little favours or nudging work in your direction, or casually mention in passing that you're good to work with. So there's little to no medium or long-term value in doing a deal where you've screwed the other side over. They might agree to your terms knowing that it's their only option and then go bust anyway, they might cut corners on the specification to make it fit, they might deliberately but subtly sabotage the product without you knowing. You might not ever know they got their own back and what it cost you. It should be a win-win situation for both parties, or at least a fair enough fair enough situation. How much damage might you do to your own future prospects by behaving badly? If you do someone a favour they may well do you one back one day. Not always, of course – there are always those who'll regard concessions as weakness, competitors as enemies and opportunities as potential for exploitation – but on balance there's more to be gained by supporting and helping other people than by being dismissive.

A relevant digression into behavioural science that I can slightly foggily remember from my zoology studies at Oxford several decades ago. One of the most basic game theories out there is that of hawks and doves, first discussed in a paper called 'The Logic of Animal Conflict', by John Maynard Smith (who I think I was lucky enough to have some lectures by) and George

Price. In competition for a limited resource, hawks always fight, and doves always back down (interestingly in the wild doves can be very aggressive and hawks often back down from conflict). There are generally considered to be three possible outcomes depending on the combination of the participants. It's usually assumed that the value gain of the payoff is less than the cost of a fight.

- If a hawk meets a hawk then each hawk will win half the time and lose half the time (assuming that they're of equal strength). One takes a beating, one gains everything.
- If a hawk meets a dove then the dove backs off, losing only the resource and the hawk takes everything.
- And if a dove meets a dove then they end up with half each.

The actual theory can get a lot more complex than this and the outcome analysis depends on many other factors, such as the relative value of the resource being fought over as compared to the cost of losing it, for example if winning means a meal and losing means dying, and the role of bluffing and patience, as well as presignalling, but those don't alter the central point – that the only way for both parties to guarantee walking away with something is for them to be doves.

You can't have a successful negotiation without some level of trust, and time spent developing this is rarely time wasted. This doesn't have to be in a work environment, and indeed arguably shouldn't be. There's a reason so many business executives play golf, after all: it's a non-workplace activity, it allows plenty of time to talk, and you can tell a lot about someone by the way they play golf – their propensity to cheat, how easily they'll concede a putt, and so on. I don't play golf, and sadly most people I negotiate with aren't prepared to settle things by a friendly joust or two, but the principle remains the same. I have a colleague who swears by the value of playing poker with colleagues. He happens to be a very good and analytical player, but he says he mostly gains insight into the way people's brains work, and keeps that in mind when negotiating with them. Poker is apparently a very disarming game and people forget that how they play and what they do gives insight into their mental processes. Personally I'm not very good at it and people seem to get annoyed when I ask what the rules are and what will beat what.

That trust can be built up over the course of negotiation by mutually reinforcing behaviour, which often means imitating your opponent's last move. If they concede on a point, they will expect you to concede on one in return – no-one likes to give something without getting something else back – and if you don't this could damage the overall trust: so if possible I try to concede back with something appropriate, but always keeping an eye on my red lines, those things I will not give way on, and if crossed means there's no deal. I've sometimes come across people who think red lines are just slightly stronger negotiating tactics, and for some people maybe they are, but not for me. If something's a red line, it's inviolable and a few very senior movie studio executives have had me walk away on a deal because of that.

An English longbowman of the Middle Ages would have special arrows with extra fluffy fletchings called flu flus, which were designed to fly a shorter distance than normal. They'd use them tactically: they'd shoot them at the enemy as a sighting and ranging arrow. The ignorant enemy would then form up just beyond the flu flus' maximum range. Assuming the archer's nerve held, they'd wait until the enemy was settled and feeling almost ready to advance, at which point the archers would switch to normal arrows and cause havoc, with both surprise and confusion. Business can be like that too. You might negotiate hard on an area which is a pinch point for them, and then you get what you want on another area which is more important to you. Not every aspect of every deal is of equal importance to both parties. In Hollywood and the film and TV industries, both of which are mostly run by freelance people (freelance meaning a knight's company who is unattached to a Lord by the way, so it's a very appropriate term for us to use here), how you get credited means a lot to people as their next job and career progression may depend on it. From my perspective I don't really care what label people put on my contributions, within reason, so I can be more flexible and less pushy in that area than others might care to be.

Constructive tension is by no means a bad thing if kept within limits. Some people wait until the very last minute before saying, 'Actually, we're still not happy about this bit,' in order to try and bounce you into giving way on a part of the deal in order to save the whole. As far as I'm concerned, that's not constructive tension: that's negotiation by ambush, and that in turn is being a dickhead. It's a shitty technique and I hate it. You see the same in buying and selling houses with gazumping and gazundering. I don't care if they're legal. They're not moral or decent ways to behave, not if you've been negotiating in good faith up till then. You have a right to expect that the other side isn't going to pull the rug from under your feet, and by the same token you have a responsibility not to do that to them.

I always try to be clear in my own head about what I want to achieve as a minimum before I enter a negotiation. Sure, there are always opportunities along the way to explore unforeseen avenues and if need be alter course a little, but there's a difference between doing that while still keeping a defined end goal in mind and just winging it, playing it by ear and making it up as you go along. It also helps to take notes and do little calculations to check numbers too. I usually have a battle plan in mind, though that approach also depends on the kind of people I'm dealing with and how the initial discussions or skirmishes progress. It's not hard to work out whether the other side are genuinely passionate about what they do or whether they're only concerned with the numbers – a version, perhaps, of Oscar Wilde's definition of the cynic as someone who knows the price of everything and the value of nothing.

Negotiators concerned with the numbers will almost certainly apply a well-worn 'secret' MBA technique to maximise immediate revenue: being 300% out from where they want to end up (demanding three times or offering a third, depending on whether they're selling or buying) and then when they come down to a position that's still faintly absurd they bank on you being so relieved that you take it. This technique is called anchoring and depends for its power on one of the many human brain glitches. Generally gain is a third as impactful as loss, so anchoring someone on a super silly price initially means than when the price is merely quite silly, we think we're getting a bargain. This works with high end fashion and handbags spectacularly well so I'm told. With those who care and are passionate, you may have to work hard to bypass their understandable sentiment and emotion clouding a realistic value, but you also have a better chance of going back to basics and saying, 'Forget the numbers on the table from either side: let's see what this is really worth.' The value of something is ultimately controlled by perception: pricing is psychology rather than economics, despite what economists would like us to believe abut rational decision making (which almost nobody does ever). Sometimes I've even negotiated with someone who's leaving that company and clearly wants to sabotage it on their way out, which is... interesting and awkward in equal measure.

It's important to try to see the world through your competitor's eyes: to position yourself where he is on the battlefield rather than where you are, to see what he can see and, just as importantly, what he can't. Knights would often have open-face visors if not facing the prospect of an arrow storm for this very reason: they could see and hear much more. Seeing a threat and moving out of the way before it strikes you is better than the most expensive armour money can buy. A business colleague told me a story about a negotiation in which they were the seller. The other side finally asked them to quote a price. My contact considered what they thought they might get, tripled it and asked for that – and the other side accepted it at once much to their surprise and delight. On one hand, you could argue that my contact had done better than they expected, but they hadn't really: all it showed was that they'd misjudged the other side's intentions, as Side B would clearly have gone much higher if they'd accepted the first offer without hesitation. Side A had committed the cardinal sin of not placing themselves in their opponents' shoes and of not seeing the bigger picture. Yes it was a win, but it could have been an even bigger win and both sides would have been happy. Some people collect stamps, personally I couldn't care less about them, but I know others care greatly and I admire them for that. Similarly I love horses and they don't. A rare stamp would be super important to them, but literally unimportant to me, and I suppose a magnificent horse would be wasted on them. The value of something depends on perceptions; if it didn't nobody would bother buying most modern art.

Even sports teams work on this: the England team which won the 2003 Rugby World Cup spent a lot of time in training on visualising the pitch from above, and the Manchester United team of the same era would do drills when they would be asked to freeze in the middle of a move and describe everything they could see. If their body placement was wrong, their field of vision would be restricted and/or include aspects which were irrelevant to the task in hand (seeing too much of the stands, for example, rather than the pitch itself). It's important to maximise not just your vision but the usefulness of that vision, and the effort of changing a viewpoint is often very much worth the energy.

I've got a reputation for being difficult because I'm lucky enough to be able to walk away from a deal on principle when I'm not happy. In many ways not needing to have to do a deal gives you power that is unassailable in the negotiation. Big companies in particular assume you won't walk away from a deal with them, because they're big and powerful, and to be fair to them they're usually right. As a result it's a surprise to them when you do. I've also had people think that my stubbornness on certain points is a way of getting more money when it's not: I'm stubborn about those points because they're important to me. If the other aspects of the deal don't fit then you can offer as much money as you like: I still won't budge. There's great strength in not giving a toss: that way you can't be pushed around against your will. For example, I don't like to give up underlying rights, no matter how much cash you throw at me. You can have a licence and the details of that we'll negotiate, but I don't want you to own the IP and lock it up for eternity. People show me their walls of 'success', all the things they've optioned – but unless those things have been made, that's not success, that's a wall of shame, of failure and wasted effort and unfulfilled dreams.

I try to think of my absolute points of no return as wildwoods. In medieval terms wildwoods were defensive flanks: fallen trees and obstacles left deliberately unmanaged as a deterrent to the enemy. If I have an area on which I simply won't compromise any further, that's a wildwood: the other side aren't making any progress through here come what may.

Sometimes, for our big bespoke game deals, I've found that people will just send along a variation on one of their standard contracts and expect some minor negotiation before it's signed: but from my point of view, that contract has been so manifestly unfit for purpose that a few tweaks on small issues are really going to make little difference. Standard contracts can be fine and fair, but sometimes, in these more complex circumstances, I've had no problem ripping the entire thing up and going back to the drawing board, starting from the basics. How much work are you putting in? How much work am I putting in? What risk lies where? Then let's apportion the return fairly. That way you can build the contract from scratch, from the ground up, rather than trying to fit it into a pre-apportioned box. 'It's our standard contract,' is usually met with, 'Here's my standard answer to that… No.'

The same is true when there's a legal logjam and progress seems to be at an impasse. The lawyers will often be arguing about individual words or tiny technical details, but that's sometimes them not seeing the wood for the trees (though equally, you could argue that they're only doing their job). In such situations I'll try to take a step back and work out what the other party is trying to achieve. The words that are causing such problems: what do they *mean*? What are you trying to protect? Your brand, for example? OK: then let's see how we can do that. If this document's not describing what we need to be describing, let's change it so that it is. Weirdly it seems some people are reluctant to say why they want something in a contract, even though often that makes sense and can be accommodated. I think they believe it shows weakness for some reason; when explaining why you need a protective term or a warranty for example, it often makes sense and therefore can go in the contract.

Despite all this, sometimes you come up against someone so far outside your comfort zone that they're not worth dealing with: people who, like the tale of the fox and the scorpion, will happily destroy themselves too, because that's their nature. With those people, and with other types of psychopath (let's be honest here, that's what you're dealing with, given something like two to five percent of people are psychopaths apparently, a number which increases or decreases with business area), there's just no crossover in communication or methodology of doing business. Mostly they fail, but sometimes they succeed and again everyone takes this as an example of how to be successful. Somebody wins the lottery almost every week after all and it's not because they're good at choosing numbers. There's a lot of media and selection bias at work here: X is aggressive and successful, therefore their success is portrayed as being down to their aggression. But as any statistician will tell you, correlation does not equal causation. Maybe X is successful despite that aggression rather than because of it: maybe X would be appreciably more successful still if they weren't so aggressive. We all probably know the story of the heavy smoker who lived into their eighties and proudly said smoking never hurt them (despite the statistics clearly showing it kills pretty much everybody else). I usually say I wonder how long they'd have lived if they didn't smoke: ninety, one hundred or more?

I've come across this in big ways and small. When people play silly buggers it's counter-productive. I've had people refuse to give me a redline mark-up of a contract, which makes it easy to see what's been changed. They've just sent a pdf instead. It makes no real odds to my reading of the contract, it's just inconvenient and frankly ruddy rude – I'll just go through it slowly and see what's been changed – but it had made me annoyed, which in turn made me determined to be more aggressive and assertive in the negotiation. But I've also had to remind myself of another truism of negotiation and medieval warfare alike: never surround an enemy so there isn't an exit available to them. Always leave them a retreat, otherwise they'll fight to the death, and it's much harder to fight someone to the death than someone who's retreating and prepared to cut their losses.

Even when the other side genuinely wants a deal, it pays to be wise to techniques they might use to soften you up. More than one supermarket representative has gone to negotiate terms with a meat supplier and found that the route to the meeting place has taken them straight through the slaughterhouse, which is no place for the faint-hearted and leaves most people quite shaken the first time they encounter it. One senior buyer in the book trade was notorious for scheduling meetings for 5pm on a Friday in a stuffy room with no air-conditioning, calculating (usually correctly) that everyone else would be so desperate to get out of there that they'd agree to practically anything. On a similar note, there's a sales technique called 'anchoring', which I mentioned before. A shop might put two handbags in the window, one costing £250,000 and the other £5,000. The latter will therefore appear to be a total bargain, even though (a) £5,000 is still a ludicrous of money for a handbag and (b) it may not even be objectively worth that amount of money.

You also have to be wise to cultural differences. A British unit was wiped out during World War II because when they radioed for help they said they were 'in a spot of bother'. The Americans on the other end of the radio took the phrase literally, figured the request wasn't urgent and allocated resources elsewhere. This is obviously an extreme example of how mismatch in communication strategies can cause problems, but the principle remains the same: be careful that what you're saying is also what the other side is hearing. One important note: it's almost impossible to both talk and listen, so ideally have one person who's a good talker and one person who can watch and listen and take notes. The way people speak can be as informative as what they're saying, and tone of language is a layer of communication.

The Japanese have pre-meetings to agree everything beforehand and work out what the meeting proper will be about. They don't want any disagreement in that meeting proper as they would consider it rude, and they don't want to offend by saying 'no' – but equally they have several different qualities of 'yes'. Negotiations can be difficult across cultural barriers, though I've always found – perhaps a little amusingly – that nothing reinforces national stereotypes like the way people do business. People from the USA are forthright and loud to the point sometimes of being actually shouty, and they hate silence, sometimes filling it with a concession in the negotiation, because a silence is worse than giving something away in the deal. The Japanese are completely the opposite, silence and few hand movements are a mark of respect; the Chinese are somewhere in the middle. The Japanese use silence a lot, usually to think about something (or at least pretend to think about it, who knows). As a result, they don't get unsettled by silence, whereas Americans do. Silence when negotiating with Americans is very powerful: if I fall quiet and count to ten in my head, I guarantee that by five they will have begun speaking to fill more detail. It can more or less force the other person to give you terms rather than let the silence linger. Silence and willingness to say no are two key pillars of negotiation.

Data. The importance of data is twofold: its gathering and its interpretation. There's a story I heard which emphasises the importance of the latter in particular. Survivorship bias was first pointed out in antiquity by Diagoras of Melos and more recently by Abraham Wald. During World War II the US Army would track all the damage to planes returning from bombing raids. They'd mark up where the most damage had been inflicted by anti-aircraft fire – on the wings, the tail, the fuselage, wherever – and then suggest that they should go to work on armouring all these areas. Until, that was, Abraham and colleagues from Columbia University pointed out the not-so-obvious: that these planes had all returned from their sorties despite the damage, so by definition that damage was non-critical (or at least non-fatal). But the planes that hadn't made it back, no-one knew what kind of damage they'd suffered: by definition there was no data on those planes. The sensible thing to do, therefore – indeed, the only proper logical conclusion – was to armour the areas that *hadn't* been hit rather than the ones that had.

Subtle effects and misunderstanding data can skew decisions badly. When we were designing the front cover for *Sniper Elite*, we put some sample covers out there for feedback. We'd divide the image into nine sectors, the way a smartphone camera does for the image it's presenting, and ask people to choose their favourite part of the image. What came back shocked us: the ugliest part of the image was the most popular, and by a margin so huge that it couldn't have been a mistake or a statistical blip. We couldn't understand, so we drilled down a bit and asked the respondents what exactly they'd found so appealing. It turned out that the vast majority of the survey had been conducted in the USA, and the respondents there had just selected the sector with the enormous gun. They didn't give two hoots for the aesthetics: they just wanted weaponry, and the bigger the better. So we used the biggest gun possible, but with good aesthetics. You must always be prepared to ask the second or third question if need be; some people even suggest going as far as asking why five times in a row to get to the real core of the answer.

Too many businesses try to anticipate future trends based on only a selected set of data. It's like relying on Nostradamus to predict the future: he put out enough predictions so that by the law of averages some of them would come true, and in addition he used obscure language so that people could take what they wanted from it. That kind of obscure language is a real charlatan's charter, irrespective of the field it appears in, and business is no exception. Analysts and PR people can couch vague waffle in marketing speak which sounds convincing but actually means nothing: they can also pick up on what you want to hear (or what they think you want to hear) and tailor their message accordingly. These nonsense phrases have been coined 'deepity' by Daniel Dennet in 2009. They are phrases that sound wise and meaningful superficially, and can fool the willingly credulous. You need to make some mental effort to unravel them and realise it's utter tripe and nonsense at its core though superficially true.

You only have to see mediums, card readers and magicians in action to know how this is done. Cold reading, where the performer will tell you all about yourself, might look and sound impressive, but when you break it down it's a mix of the bleeding obvious and some serious verbal legerdemain. If

I'm the performer and you're the target, I'll be able to tell quite a lot about you even before you open your mouth – your age, your appearance, the way you dress – and even more once you start talking (your accent). Then all I have to do is ask you basic questions and let you fill in the rest of the details yourself.

To anyone in middle age or above, for example, the question 'Have you lost someone close to you lately?' is almost bound to receive an answer in the affirmative, simply because middle-aged people will either have friends who've died relatively young or elderly relatives whose time was up. It's not a sign of communication with the spirit world to know this: it's an educated guess which almost always pays dividends. 'I'm getting a message from your... aunt? Your uncle? He died... this year? The last few weeks?' Talk about hedging your bets. There's a name coming through from the other side. The name begins with a letter, it might be an H, it's a bit hazy, keep trying to come though, or it might be an F, no it's a J or yes, that's it. Someone shouts, 'It's Aunty Ethel', the cold reader or medium agrees yes it's Ethel, she says how are you and she has a message for you... and so on.

But people love to believe that stuff, and so the unscrupulous can take advantage of it. The magician's choice is a similar example. A magician has a pack of cards split into two, and they need to keep a specific one of those halves known to them, so they ask you to choose. If you choose the correct one, they say, 'Let's keep this': if you choose the wrong one they say 'Let's discard this.' You'd be surprised how often this can apply in life. You really need to know what the outcome of each choice is before you make that choice, or it's not really a choice at all. I try as far as possible to eliminate bias, unconscious or otherwise, as much as possible before making a decision: to see who or what is pulling the wool over my eyes and whether

94

they mean to or not. It's hard to do and I'm sure I fail a lot, but trying and failing and trying again is very knightly and chivalrous.

Bad data is often worse than no data. Publishing, for example, relies greatly on Nielsen BookScan figures, which track sales of every published book and is therefore a vital tool for publishers, retailers, authors and agents. The problem comes when this data is used without regard for its limitations. An author who writes a book which sells poorly may well find that publishers are more reluctant to sign future books from them, not least because those publishers know that retailers may well also be spooked by those poor figures and therefore order fewer copies, which means less visibility for that author, which means fewer sales, and so the circle continues to narrow.

But this ignores the simple fact that an author's previous sales don't necessarily predict their future ones, and the potential reader doesn't care a hoot. They have no visibility of this data. There can be any number of reasons for a book's poor sales which have nothing to do with the quality of the book: poor marketing, saturated market, bad timing, controversial subject, bad cover, and so on. None of those might apply to the next book, which could be in a completely unrelated genre: so to base a decision about that book on factors which may be only tangentially related at best seems otiose. And we all know badly written books that have sold well too.

To someone with a hammer, everything is a nail. BBC viewing figures, for example, are based on a relative handful (I think about 15,000) of households who are tasked with clicking on a device to register what they're watching, and the figures are then scaled up using statistical methods. But the numbers can easily be skewed, not just in the act of scaling (which is by definition as an estimate, inaccurate) but also because production companies might know who's on the list and might therefore, potentially, encourage people to misrepresent what they watch (which would be deliberate error) or people forget to record what they were watching and just make something up. The margin for error is likely to be very significant, and scaling that up to cover the population just compounds that error. Imagine having to make strategic decisions on the battlefield if you don't know how many troops you have or where they are with any degree of accuracy. Sir Bob, one of a thousand knights, is still alive and fighting well, so that means everybody else is still alive. Compare this to Netflix or YouTube and other similar data streaming services, who have real-time figures not just of what's being seen but how long it's shown for and which sections are paused or re-watched. They don't know if somebody is actually looking at the screen, or exactly how many people are, or if they're concentrating or if the show is 'on in the background', but they know an order of magnitude more than the old-style broadcasters. They know that data in real time, and they can see that data change moment by moment. They then feed this data back into production decisions. I imagine one of their biggest issues is working out why something is popular or not, and I bet those decisions are packed with human biases. This show is successful because actor X is in it, and he's great. Alternatively the show's title sounds interesting, or the thumbnail (the little image advertising it) is very well made, and it had nothing to do with that actor. These things are very hard to tease out of the data without multifactor testing. (My educated guess here is that there's a disappointing amount of randomness in the success or failure of something.)

The BBC is largely populated, certainly at executive level, by self-identified left-leaning university-educated people who are tasked with making choices for a very broad demographic but don't know, with much confidence, what people choose to watch. Data for commercial content creators should be very important, and that can only come not from what people say but what they actually do. It's well known that people say things others want to hear. There was a case in the US when a cable TV company tracked the viewing habits of a religious community and found that quite a few housewives were watching porn in the middle of the day – but when they questioned these women in a probably very awkward, face-to-face survey, every single one flatly denied it of course. We've all been stopped in the street and in a moment of madness agreed to answer a few questions. If the questioning goes on too long and they've stretched people's tolerance, on occasion I believe people might just make up untrue answers... maybe.

A business needs good knowledge to help it move from one way of doing things to another, and in doing so to stay fresh, viable and solvent. In any business you can get to the top of a small hill and find that you've perfected what you've done to get there. In evolutionary terms that's known as a local maxima. But then the market moves to the next, bigger hill, and you have to try to get there. The bit that people aren't prepared for is to go down into the valley en route, to make mistakes and perhaps even see productivity decline, before starting the next ascent.

We've all been there in our personal lives even without realising it: we went to primary school, rose to the top there, then had to start again at the bottom of secondary school and work our way up again, and then for a third time at university. At each stage we've gone from being a big cheese to a mini Babybel, and found the standard around us rising all the time. For some people that can be psychologically devastating, but it's a progression that must be gone through: and the same applies in business. In chemistry they call it initiation energy, the energy put in to make something happen better and faster eventually. If you don't put that energy in you'll only stay at your local maximum, where things are only as good as they need to be for the current circumstances.

On the other hand, there's a difference between a local maximum and a practicable wider maximum. Good enough, providing that it's on a sufficiently large scale, is often just that, good enough. It's easy to want to be a perfectionist and make everything as wonderful as it can be, but in practical terms that's either not going to happen or is going to cost more than it gains. The old adage, 'Don't let the best be the enemy of the good,' is a wise one here. Even in terms of market ranking you're statistically unlikely to be the best, but if you can be even marginally better than the average then you're winning.

There's another old saying, since we're on the subject of pithy clichés, that you should 'be first, be best or be cheapest', but of those I think numbers one and three aren't necessarily true, and number two should read 'better' rather than 'best'. Just as middle distance runners prefer to be the one on the leader's shoulder rather than the leader themself, so too can it be an advantage to see where the first ones in have made mistakes. Google wasn't the first search engine, Facebook wasn't the first digital diary. Bill Gates was smart and counter-intuitive, and probably a bit lucky too, by choosing to focus on software, not hardware, at a time when everyone else was building machines. Having said that, making hardware would have probably required far too much investment to compete with the manufacturing giants, so software may have actually been the only viable route. If anybody tells you luck played no part in their success, they're fibbing. It's how you build on your good luck, and how you deal with bad luck, that informs success.

Being better, and having long-term success, can also depend on two other things. The first is spreading the risk via diversification. This goes for any portfolio, whether that is your own personal shareholdings or what your company works on. At Rebellion we have our 'bankers' like the various games in the *Sniper Elite* and *Zombie Army* series, but we can't just rely on those as at some stage all empires fall, just ask the Romans (though to be fair the Eastern Roman Empire lasted a very long time indeed). So we have to innovate, but equally we choose not to risk throwing everything at innovation. Some people are happy doing that, maybe they have a higher threshold for gambling, or maybe we only hear about the very few successes that this drives; after all, people rarely spend money on publicising their failures (remember survivor bias). There will always be risk: it's controlling and managing that risk which is essential. Just as a medieval lord was responsible for leading a whole host of people and their livelihoods on his manor, so too is any company owner and executive responsible for their staff and those livelihoods, and it's incumbent on those people in power to behave with everyone's best interests at heart and not simply stake everything on a mad gamble. Those mad gambles do come off, of course, and when they do they receive a lot of attention, but that in itself is confirmation bias: they fail far more often than they succeed, and the failures don't attract anything like the same amount of attention. That's why slot machines make a huge fanfare when someone wins but stay silent when they lose: they want to keep people pouring in money in the hope that the next fanfare will be theirs. (Note that there's no negative equivalent of the fanfare, often not even a sad tone or a thumbs down, just silence and nothing, they literally don't want to draw attention to failure.)

The second involves accepting that no business is totally shockproof or futureproof. Oceanographers know that out at sea sometimes, very occasionally, vast wave peaks of 100 feet or more can just appear (in fact, these might be the origins of folk tales about sea monsters such as the Kraken), and of course with 100-foot peaks come 100-foot troughs: both of them the result of a myriad unseen forces in deep-running currents which come to a head at a single point in space and time. They are the very occasional superposition of peaks or troughs of the normally out-of-sync wave forms that make up the surface of the sea. So too the case with business. That perfect wave can appear and affect you for no other reason than that you're there. It can pick you up and lift you to vast success, or it can crash over you and bury you. Luck, both good and bad, has a huge effect on fortunes, but people often only admit that when the luck has worked against them. There's no shame in admitting you got fortunate: it's crucial and admirable to do so, not embarrassing, and also suggests that you have a clear-eyed view of your business.

On the flip side, thousands of perfectly good businesses were blindsided by Covid, a once-in-a-century pandemic. Take a well-known UK chain of urban sandwich bars with a French name. Obviously I don't know the ins and outs of its business model, but it seemed predicated on fairly sound assumptions: that millions of workers with disposable income come flooding into central London every day, and since they're both busy and used to high standards they'll pay good money for delicious takeaway food. And then the pandemic comes along and not just suspends normal working patterns for a year or so – that's the bit that's almost easy to deal with – but threatens to alter them forever even after the pandemic has subsided: and suddenly all those assumptions look way off piste. Yet there were really no underlying structural flaws in them, just a black swan event which has turned so much of conventional wisdom on its head. Sure, you can adjust in advance for such an event, but only at the expense of altering your normal business practices to such an extent that they will begin to work against you unless and until the catastrophe you've been predicting takes place. Whatever you can anticipate and plan for, rest unassured (sic) that there are other things you have not planned for, or even conceived of, that can pop up and will have to be dealt with in real time.

Behaviour. There are techniques from gameplay which can be used to encourage better business behaviour, if only businesses were prepared to use them. I once discussed this with HMRC, the British tax people, who, as always, were looking to get tax in as early as possible. I said, 'OK, then give people an incentive. If you get your tax in three months early, you get one percent off it: if six months early, two percent.' They couldn't fathom that. They said, 'What if everyone gets it in early?' 'Then modify it,' I said. 'Change it to a prize draw entry for £10,000, or give an incentive for referring other people to this system.' They still couldn't fathom. They were so wedded to their existing system, which offered no reward but only punishment (fines for being late), that they couldn't see that they were missing some of the toolbox.

That said, research shows that loss aversion is at least four times more powerful than gain reward. Personally I think it's much more than that, but let's go with the data. If you are designing a game where you want someone to keep something, the best way is to give it to them before taking it away and charging them money to get it back: they're much more likely to pay than if you'd asked for payment up front. The French philosopher Alexis de Tocqueville said something similar about society at large: that revolutions happen not when people have nothing, but when they've had something and it's been taken away from them.

When you're jousting, it's easy to focus just on your opponent's eye slot, or occulorum, and miss the other signs of what they might be about to do: their arms, body language, position in the saddle and so on can all give you perhaps a better clue as to their intentions, and of course watching their horse too can furnish more information. Adrenaline literally causes tunnel vision. So is it too in business: if you fixate on just one thing you can find yourself going wrong. Smart people make you see what they want you to see. Try to consider what they're not telling you. The same phenomenon of restricted vision has been reported in various other arenas: combat veterans often experience some sort of tunnel vision, and even high-standard chess players have sometimes found themselves concentrating so hard on one particular corner of the board where the current action is that they've missed threats from afar and/or their opponent swinging an attack across to the other side. There's that famous experiment which you can find on YouTube, where a group of people are passing a beach ball among themselves and you're asked to count how many passes they make. You're so focussed on counting that you don't see a man in a gorilla suit walking slowly through the players, even stopping to wave at the camera! The second time you watch the clip you can't believe you missed it, but that's the point.

The mind is an easy thing to mislead. We're all used to the phenomenon when you suddenly start hearing lots of things about, say, Queen Victoria, which you haven't before. The truth is that the frequency of these occurrences hasn't usually increased: it's just that your brain has latched onto one instance and started building patterns around it. The media do similar around things such as stabbings and fires, making instances sound like some sort of sudden epidemic when underlying figures simply don't bear this out. It happens in the animal world too: a fox will mooch around until it gets hungry and decides it wants blackberries to eat. It will then focus relentlessly on finding blackberries until either there are no more blackberries or it's no longer hungry.

In zoology one, obviously, studies animals, but also what animals do and research into why they do what they do. After all, brains have evolved alongside bodies, and what brains tell bodies to do has a big effect on survival of both, but sometimes this biological 'software' is imperfect, or perhaps I should say good enough to deal with most things, but not with everything. Amongst other research, we learned about animal behaviour and Skinner boxes. In this case (and in summary which might cause my professors to sigh with exasperation), pigeons' behaviour was studied to see what effect rewards of tiny amounts of grain had on their behaviour. It started with simple correlation: a pigeon would tap a lever and find a piece of grain being delivered. But gradually Skinner decoupled action and reward: sometimes a tap would lead to grain, and sometimes not. The pigeon's behaviour would become more extreme the more this went on: it would spin around and do all kinds of weird things until the tap/grain correlation was restored, even temporarily. When the intervals between rewards were entirely random, bizarre rituals would start to emerge, even though the behaviour was not linked to the reward. In essence, the pigeon was doing what humans do with myths, folklore and conspiracy theories: trying to influence and explain random behaviour by making a story of its own, and in doing so hoping to impose some sort of control on its external environment. Imagine this scenario: the village shaman says it will rain tomorrow if you all give him some nice food, you do, and it rains. Everybody is happy. He says the same thing next time there's a drought, and you give him food again but it doesn't rain. He says it's because you didn't give the right sort of food in the right way, so he's not at fault, you are, for 'doing it wrong' or not believing in him enough. You follow his instructions and eventually it rains again, proving the shaman is in control of the rain, and voila, early religion. Human brains are great at finding patterns, but the software errs on the side of over recognition, as it pays off to correlate false positives more easily than false negatives: you can see this with athletes and their superstitions (lucky pants, order of entry onto the pitch, etc). But unless they win every time then the correlation of superstition with result is a flawed one. Over recognition of patterns makes sense if you think of the relative risks and rewards in this oversimplified scenario. If you detect that there's a tiger in the bushes and run away, either there is one and you ran away or there wasn't one and you used up some energy and time running away; no big deal really, maybe you feel a little silly. If you don't detect that there's a tiger in the bushes and there is one, and you ignore it, you're eaten and dead. Over-pattern recognition is a survival trait, but leads to conspiracy theories and over correlation.

In the Olympics, certain sports of aggression – boxing, wrestling, taekwondo – are fought between competitors assigned red and blue kit, and these are randomised as red has been shown to make the wearer more aggressive. Statistically speaking those wearing red kit win slightly more than those wearing blue kit if everything else is controlled for. Goalkeepers in football/soccer have also found that wearing very bright, fluorescent colours draws the eye of opposing strikers unconsciously and therefore prompts them to shoot nearer them, meaning a slightly higher chance of intercepting the ball before a goal is scored. In times past certain goalkeepers would wear black, which is intimidating, but could also make it counter-intuitively easier for the opposing players to score as they'd look for the light around it.

The human brain is good at recognising patterns, especially with practice. Chess provides good examples of this. There was an experiment done once where players of varying ability, from near-beginners to grandmasters, were shown various positions and given a minute to study each of them before reconstructing that position from memory. In positions that had been taken from games the grandmasters fared much better than everyone else, but in positions that had been randomly generated – i.e. the kind of positions which would never occur in any vaguely feasible match scenario – the gap was much smaller. The reason was simple: chess has certain patterns to it, certain often-found piece structures or groupings, which experienced players perceive not as individual pieces but as a single entity, making it easier to recognise and remember. In complex positions, where computer search engines (now much stronger than even the best human players) will calculate the best positions fundamentally through brute force at lightning speed, top grandmasters will after a certain point rely on intuition: a move will feel right, perhaps even smell right.

Even small behavioural points can have far-reaching effects:

- You need to have your wits about you even in what can appear to be benign situations. In an interview, journalists sometimes ask easy questions first to soften you up, then drop in a difficult one and trust that you're suitably in the flow of the interview and/ or feeling receptive to answer it in a way which may be more revealing than you would ideally like. Or, if they're using a remote mic on TV or in a conference setting, they ask you after the main body of the interview when you assume that the mic is off and the recording has stopped. Remote wireless microphones are very easy to forget you're wearing, and forgetting you're actively broadcasting sound to the sound crew when you pop to the toilet is a hazard of being a presenter.

• Very few things are so urgent that you need to do them *right now*: there's almost always time to pause and be absolutely sure you want to take the proposed course of action. That's perhaps easier said than done in a world of instant communication, but that in turn makes this arguably more rather than less important: once it's out there you can't call it back. Whenever I'm going to send an important e-mail, I don't just check it through before sending, but I also like to wait a while – a few hours, perhaps even a day. Is the tone the one I want to get across? Are there bits I should soften? Do I need to be blunter at certain points? Is it all clear? Are any parts confusing? I get things wrong sometimes: everyone does. And when I do, I try to rectify things. But it seems to me that people increasingly like to double down on being wrong. You point out where they're mistaken and they just won't have it. Maybe they just like the endorphin rush of the argument, I don't know. There's certainly a section of the social media-consuming public who seem to relish attention and don't care how they get it. If they have to troll people mercilessly, then so be it. In times past you could ring on someone's doorbell and run away before they answered. Now you don't even need to let go of your smartphone to have the same effect.

- Don't be afraid to say you don't understand. It's not a sign of weakness or stupidity. I once had someone explain a complex tax scheme to me. He explained the first time and I didn't get it, so I asked him to explain it again. Second time round, I still didn't get it. It was a little embarrassing. Third time round, after I asked a couple of supplementary questions, I finally got it, because I realised it wasn't a legitimate tax scheme at all: it was dodgy, or it seemed dodgy to me. In the following few years the tax authorities convinced the courts it was dodgy too, costing some very famous people some significant sums of money in the process. I'm sure the terms used in court were more technical than dodgy, but they meant the same thing.

Finally, humanity's ability to do things has usually run ahead of the capacity to decide whether or not we should do them. There was a photograph taken in 2019 of the queue to reach the summit of Everest: scores of people lined up on the high slopes of the mountain as though they were shoppers securing their place in line for the opening of the January sales. It was almost impossible to look at that photo and not feel a sense of unease. It's less than seventy years since Everest was first climbed, and in the footsteps of those first two intrepid, brave and incredibly skilled men, Edmund Hillary and Tensing Norgay, have come thousands of others, many of them looking to change their own lives or at least find some deeper meaning in them: and so you get that photograph.

What that photograph *doesn't* show is the carnage which many of those climbers reported that day: people stepping round dead bodies without a second glance, pushing and shoving to take selfies. One climber called it 'a zoo: *Lord of the Flies* at 29,000 feet'. Another said he 'saw some people like they had no emotions. I asked people for water and no one gave me any. People are really obsessed with the summit. They are ready to kill themselves for the summit.'

That people behave like this is understandable, if not particularly edifying. The high reaches of Everest are not called the 'death zone' for nothing: oxygen cylinders only have a finite capacity; judgment can be seriously impaired. Mountaineering by definition is a selfish, obsessional pursuit: it has to be. And for all those who wax lyrical about finding their grace up in that wafer-thin air, there are as many whose motivation is the simpler 'because it's there'.

The other thing that photograph does not show is that many of those climbers are relatively inexperienced. It's not true to say that 'anyone can climb Everest' – you need to be very fit and possess exceptional mental strength – but it is true that you don't need advanced climbing skills in the way you do to attempt, say, K2. Some of the climbers here reportedly didn't even know how to use basic mountain equipment such as crampons and ice axes.

This inexperience is what helps cause delays: climbers needing to follow the lead of others, or unable to respond quickly to situations which arise. If you want to compete in the Hawaii Ironman, you need to qualify. If you want to race motorbikes, you need a licence. But if you want to climb Everest, all you need is the money, the time and the will.

It's easy to point fingers: at the Nepali government, for making as much money as they can out of issuing permits without any kind of expertise level being necessary; at the myriad of unscrupulous tour operators determined to get their clients up there fastest; at the environmental damage to a fragile ecosystem all the way from Base Camp up; and at the rise of social media which both fuels and reflects the spirit of extreme challenge.

It's much harder to know how to solve these. How else is a poor country with an incredibly lucrative resource going to behave? How else are operators in an unregulated market going to survive and thrive? How to stop or reverse this damage without also losing the golden calf of those who pay handsomely to cause it? How else are people seeking to push themselves further and further going to do this? There are questions, but no firm answers. The one thing that's for sure is the one thing which is always true about human progress: that it cuts both ways, and that our capacity to do things almost always outweighs our capacity to decide whether or not we should do them. There's a very dark meme about Everest which goes as follows: 'Every dead body on Mount Everest was once a highly motivated individual.'

Chapter Five

Prudence

PRUDENCE IN THE modern world tends to have financial implications: it's hard even to hear the word without thinking of dour Presbyterians standing in drizzle or Gordon Brown intoning it as an article of faith in his economic policy. (Previous generations may have associated Prudence with the Jilly Cooper book of that title or the Beatles track 'Dear Prudence', which if nothing else proves that progress can move in mysterious ways.) I try to follow the tenets of financial prudence in both my professional and personal life. Prudence is about lots of things. It's about looking after the little details. It's about going over a contract for the fifth time and double checking the small print. It's about choosing the right people to work with, choosing good partners where you can, and learning from your mistakes. But most of all for me, central to prudence is one overriding concept: independence.

There are lots of different ways of defining an independent games developer and publisher. I don't think you can get any more purely independent than we are: we're a family-owned business, literally, controlled by Chris and me. That's it, no-one else. I've always felt that being the CEO of a company with too many external shareholders is in some ways rather like being the knight chosen to carry the banner on a medieval battlefield: it's a huge honour, looks good, but it doesn't half cramp your style. The banner-bearing knight would have to control his horse with reins in one hand and carry the banner with the other, leaving no hand for a weapon. The banner was a mark of honour and a signifier of location, meaning that when the banner was furled the honour was hidden – but furled was much easier to ride with, as the weight of an unfurled banner and the way the wind could take it could cause huge problems. The knight with the unfurled banner would mark out his lord, and help rally the troops, control them and get them into formation, but he couldn't really get stuck in himself. He had no hands free to wield a weapon. His very job was to act as a focal point for his own side, and of course, as a focus point for the enemy attacks. Richard III, the last King of England to die in battle, killed Sir William Brandon, the noble banner-bearer of the Welsh usurper Henry Tudor at the Battle of Bosworth in 1485, failing to kill Henry himself and losing his own life in the battle.

As CEO of a company which is controlled entirely by Chris and me, I can get stuck in all I like and don't have to be holding a banner at the time. As CEO of a public company, I'd forever need to be carrying that banner to mark myself out to the world at large. I've been told that I'd probably need to go to investment conference after investment conference and make the same speech with minor variations. I wonder if anyone has been tempted to turn up with cymbals and a fez, just to make the performing monkey parallels obvious.

As we saw in the introduction, the other chivalric codes specifically mention the spurning of pecuniary reward. I think that means one shouldn't do things *just* for money, like a hireling or a mercenary might do. One should do them because they're worthwhile or worthy too, obviously and literally; a knight needed money to run a household, to buy and maintain several horses, arm and armour himself and his many followers and staff. Business decisions shouldn't be just about maximising revenue or return at any cost, or aimed at securing ever more external investment according to some MBA-taught share price/stock market fixation. They should be about making profits to reinvest in the company and add value in multiple ways in the medium to long term.

Some external shareholders skew a business's entire rationale and necessarily change the motivation for running that business: away from the fundamentals of the business itself and towards building up and capitalising on the confidence of external investors who don't really know anything about the company. Business schools are full of people for whom the company is the product rather than the means to make the product itself: but running a successful business is, in part, about controlling the short-term, greedy, darker aspects to human nature. Even the very concept of shares demonstrates this. They began with Italian water mills in medieval times, and involve the separation of ownership and actual work. No longer did workers produce things and get paid directly for them: instead, merchants would buy a portion of the mill, literally a share of it, and then pay the workers a wage.

But many investors run on a lot of emotion, sentiment, and gut feel, no matter what they say, or what analysts tell you, which makes their decisions and priorities even more suspect. Remember the ability of the human brain to over recognise patterns that aren't there? The example of Games Workshop is a case in point. They manufacture miniature figures for wargames such as *Warhammer*, and while they had the licence to do *Lord of the Rings* games too their share price was stratospheric and they became cash rich. In a five-year period, their turnover more than doubled, their net profit rose 600%, and their share price was up almost 2,000%. When the licence ended (which they always said it would and which they flagged well in advance) their share price collapsed, and at one stage you could have bought them for less than they had cash in the bank – which was ridiculous, because even without *Lord of the Rings* their business model (forgive the pun) was successful and their underpinnings sound. They paid dividends entirely out of surplus cash rather than debt, and their philosophy was very in tune with my own. 'We don't spend money on things we don't need, like expensive offices or prime rent shopping locations or advertising that speaks to the mass market and not our small band of loyal followers. We only invest where it makes a positive improvement to our business model.' But they still had to deal with major corporate interest – their three biggest shareholders were JP Morgan, Schroders and Standard Life.

Don't get me wrong. I'm glad to see the City and investors taking an interest in video games, not just in terms of the industry as it stands but also how it bodes for the future. However, we value our independence, we don't have any plans to float. It's very exciting for the ones who've done IPOs, like Codemasters, Sumo, Frontier and Team17 – they're colleagues and friends of mine – but they're different kinds of businesses to us, particularly now they're owned by the public. And because we have no venture capitalist or merchant bankers to cash in their shares, we can do what we want to do, and double down on the reason we set up Rebellion a long time ago, which was to do cool stuff.

We knew we wanted to build up our own IP and fund our own games, and that is where we are now. It's taken us a long time, over twenty-five years, to get here, but we now come up with the ideas, fully fund the games, and release them ourselves worldwide. Games these days aren't cheap: they cost many tens of millions of pounds to make. Some of our competitors' games costs hundreds of millions to bring to market. We're in a lucky enough position to be able to put those millions of our own back into making new games, and that our games are successful enough to generate a decent return on that investment. Being independent is about being independent in all aspects. We don't have to worry about where the investment comes from. It comes from us. And that's great: there's no-one else in the loop. We're the equivalent of a film studio in terms of computer games (but perhaps even more so as I believe most of the big film studios borrow money in complex ways to fund their movie productions, presumably in an effort to reduce their own risk). The same when it comes to comics and book publishing. We work with distributors but they never say: 'No, you can't publish that book.' Ideally, I want to be in that position when it comes to film and TV. It's clearly an ambitious thing but I don't see why we shouldn't be. Back when we first started, we relied on third parties for funds, as we were what is called a 'work-for-hire' studio. We worked on some great properties: *Star Wars, Alien vs. Predator, Harry Potter, The Simpsons, James Bond*. But we worked for other people; our output belonged to other people. We were the mill workers, not the Italian medieval mill owners. Nowadays the games we make are our own and we are beginning to build up a very respectable, globally appreciated, commercially successful portfolio of stuff: *Sniper Elite, Zombie Army, Strange Brigade* and *Evil Genius*.

At heart we're a creative business. There are two words in that simple phrase: creative and business, and you've got to consider both those elements equally. Rebellion only makes games that I'd want to play myself, which can free the development team from having to slavishly follow whatever the latest industry wave is. Some of our games target older players who aren't so keen on the competitive pressures or super fast hand-eye coordination of many modern games. I'm very keen that our games respond to the needs of all different types of players. I want a single-player experience and I want team-based multiplayer co-op. I particularly like games where you team up with friends to take on the computer-controlled enemy. That reduces game guilt for me. I love co-op multiplayer especially because it's more friendly, positive and team spirited. Head-to-head multiplayer is all very well, and hugely successful, but it can and does get very competitive and, quite frankly, as previously mentioned, I'm rubbish. I haven't got the time to play them and 'git gud', as people keep shouting at me online and as you age your ability to, and interest in, 360 no scopes and remembering the latest digital playground slang reduces markedly.

We do acquire other companies as and when it suits and when the right circumstance arises. It's not an ongoing policy: we're not going out actively looking for strategic companies to acquire. But if we work with people, and we like them, and the opportunity pops up, and it's a win-win situation for us both, then we'll look at it positively and try to do it. They're usually opportunistic: we've worked with a talented bunch of people in the past, there's an opportunity to work more closely with them again, and if we don't make those kind of moves then sooner or later someone else might.

Though the acquisitions may be opportunistic, they're not random: for example, many of the extra staff we've employed over the past few years will work on both our big tentpole productions, such as future iterations of the flagship *Sniper Elite* series, and a few smaller games as well. We've always planned the future in terms of things like how many titles should we be doing and what platforms should we be working on. When it came to dealing with nextgen, that is the newest technical generation of games consoles, Chris and I sat down and worked out that our team sizes would need to be significantly over one hundred members of staff, for likely three years or more, with budgets in the multiple millions of dollars. It would have been difficult and slow to build up team sizes to that scale organically, so the opportunity to buy entire studios, with talented staff that work well as a team, has worked out for us so far.

We've always thought having only one game in development is risky, both for the developer, if it's work-for-hire, and the publisher who is funding it. It's risky for the developer because the publisher has the power. But it's also risky for the publisher because the only option if the project goes wrong is to shoot the developer dead (metaphorically just in case you thought it might be literal, though I'm sure some publisher–developer relationships end up considering pistols at dawn). There's no middle route. We work on the principle of having roughly five projects at different stages of development on the basis that a project takes, very roughly, three years. If you want to release one or more projects a year, you need four projects in development at any one time, and a fifth one would be really good. We thought, let's aim for five sizeable projects. How many people do we need? Obviously you won't need 150 people working on a project from start to finish, so we thought it's probably something like 400–500 on payroll.

Ideally, we want to get to a position where we've got a big game coming out each year, plus one or more smaller, arguably more experimental new titles, new IP, that kind of innovation. We want to test new things out, like we did with the hugely successful *Strange Brigade*. But we've got to balance that out: we've got to keep going with *Sniper Elite* because lots of people want more *Sniper Elite*. *Sniper Elite* stands firmly alongside major franchise games like *Call of Duty*, or *Assassin's Creed*, and similar. We don't sell in numbers quite as much as they do, perhaps because we don't have the marketing muscle or the distribution muscle, but we're not far off. And if you look at our marketing budget and development and compare our return on investment with them, you'd want to be sitting in our shoes. We do very, very well. We sell games everywhere in the world, and that's exciting. We're eighty-five, maybe ninety percent export driven. I think the only country in the world where we don't have a record of selling our games is North Korea. Funnily enough we do have a record of selling a game to a place with officially zero inhabitants. It turns out to be a research base, and two people there were obviously into playing our games.

This all stems from and comes back to the fact that we're independent and control the company between us, which makes such moves far simpler than they might be for many. All we do when an opportunity comes up is look at it and go, 'Yeah, that kind of makes sense,' or, 'No, that's not for us.' We won't do millions of quids' worth of due diligence, scare ourselves and then decide not to do it. In my limited experience of them, business consultants often know a lot less about your subject than they let on, but they advise with a dispassionate perspective and a metric ton of learned confidence. We'll do a sensible amount of research, look into the data properly, and then decide between us whether we think we can make a go of it. Because we're privately owned, it's our money. Our money and our responsibility, both success and failure. We're almost unique in the games industry in being like that. There have been opportunities that have come up that we've not moved on. But because we're not publicly owned, nobody knows that those opportunities came and went and we didn't do anything about it. This puts us in a fortunate position. We don't have to manage a relationship with a complex set of investors in any way, shape or form. We try to keep nimble. We have a very small board: me and my brother and various advisors. At the end of the day if we need a decision in the afternoon we can sit down in the morning, look at the numbers and make a decision and get back to people the same day (though we usually follow our 24-hour pondering rule). We can react very quickly, but we only want to do things we want to do, and work with those we respect and get on with. Life is too short otherwise.

This flexibility has allowed us to buy motion capture studio Audiomotion, which has worked on a whole raft of big-budget movies: *Ready Player One, Star Wars: The Last Jedi, World War Z, A Monster Calls, Miss Peregrine's Home For Peculiar Children, Maleficent, Harry Potter and the Deathly Hallows, Iron Man 2*, and *Watchmen*. Although Audiomotion is our company, we've always kept it separate from Rebellion as it's used by third parties. I don't know what it's doing on a daily basis, as that might not be fair to those using it. But I know that it's solved a lot of technical problems for people in film and TV, which is good both externally (ensures a good reputation with customers) and internally (gives us confidence to know we can do our own stuff).

When we bought a vast set of buildings and turned them into a film studio based in Didcot, it was because we were looking around for where to film and realised that there just wasn't that much studio space left in the UK. The government said there was a shortfall of 2 million square feet of space, which basically meant there wasn't anywhere to film: and as newcomers we knew we'd be low down on the pecking order for facilities. I also wanted anywhere we were filming to be to be fairly local to me, because I want to be involved on a daily basis. And so in typical Rebellion fashion we thought: how do you square this circle? Can we buy somewhere? And that's how we acquired the Didcot studios. We looked around for 'big sheds' which is how we described what we wanted to the estate agents. And we've set about turning those into facilities that other people can use and we can use: we hire some of it out and use the rest ourselves. It's a huge 12-acre site: 250,000 square feet of space, really, really tall and soundproof; it couldn't be better. You could film a James Bond villain's lair in it!

But even though we do work for and with other companies, and while it's interesting talking with Hollywood executives at a very senior level, what we don't want to do, and what we're not going to do, in the main, is get back into pure work-for-hire. We don't want to reverse into a situation where we're basically doing work-for-hire for movie studios. We got out of that a decade ago in games, and we're not going back into it. What we now pursue on principle are joint ventures. We've got a significant library of fascinating intellectual property from comics, books, all sorts of stories in many genres. But we don't necessarily want to just make games from IP generated in other industries. We want to keep a balance between game IP that's going to be books, book IP that's going to be a comic, comic IP that's going to be a game. Not every idea is suitable for every game, book, comic or movie; some just work well in one or two of those. Sometimes I'm asked why we haven't made X into a game, or Y into a comic, or Z into a movie yet, and the answer is usually one of two things: we haven't got round to it yet, or we don't think it would make a good one. It's just fun to be telling stories and making games for other people to play. But Chris and I still make products that we want to consume too. I try, and sometimes succeed, to play all our games through several times from start to finish. In the early days I absolutely played them all many times over; these days I play as much of them as I can manage. We're indie in that respect, yet big enough to be able to put a huge team of talented people on a game for multiple years.

That's very much how our business is: we operate a portfolio approach to both risk and product. A lot of people say that's boring. A lot of people suggest that they like the more 'casino approach' to investing – they want to see a 100% return on their money in a year or two, which is possible but unlikely usually. There just aren't many instant returns and if someone is promising to double your money in a year, there's a good chance they could lose all your money as well. We've always tried to approach things with a distributed risk approach: if one project doesn't work as well as we hoped, never mind. Move on to the next one. We don't bet everything on one roll of the dice: that becomes gambling rather than business. One product should not be the thing that will make or break your company. We can be proactive in some areas and then reactive in others, and we do what feels best. The unsung heroes of British commerce are those who can turn a modest disaster into a modest success. Spread your risks, then the good decisions will outweigh the bad. There aren't any magic solutions to running a business, just a sensible amount of hard work. There have been overnight successes, and it is possible, usually on the public markets, to become an overnight mega success, but if you dig beneath the surface you often find out that the underlying business has either found a loophole in existing legislation, or is pumping out positive stories, with huge goodwill being generated and the shares are skyrocketing as a result of the emotions of investors. Stockmarket bubbles have existed in the past; the ones I'm familiar with go as far back as the tulip futures in the early to mid-17th century in Europe then on into the Southsea bubble of the early 18th century, then canal mania of the early 19th century, the dot com boom and ever onwards. They're getting more frequent from my inexpert viewpoint, and all feature investment hubris, followed by collapse. You can make a lot of money out of a bubble but only if you get in and out at the right time. Greed often prevents good timing.

There are advantages and disadvantages that come with a growing business. If its growth is co-ordinated properly, you end up with something where the whole is greater than the sum of the parts. For example, you can get overlap of technology: so we might be doing project A, which is a sci-fi shooter, and project B, which is a historical shooter. Some of those technology elements will be the same, so you can reuse them and then focus your production resources to really push the sci-fi and the historical aspects. In that way, both games can benefit more than if you were doing just one game at a time.

Of course there are problems that come with scaling up: there are plenty of cautionary examples of game developers such as Argonaut or Kaboom! who went bust, arguably, because they over-expanded, or so I've been led to believe by insiders who were there, though usually it's much more complicated than that in reality. Often it's several bad decisions in a row plus some bad luck thrown in just to make recovery even harder. It's easy to look at the future when things are going well and not believe that the bad times are coming, but you have to be realistic and you have to make strong, and sometimes difficult and unpleasant, management decisions early. As it is, we end up turning down loads of work. We just don't have the bandwidth. I hate turning down projects because I think people will be offended but if I don't have the people to do it, I can't do it. Partly it's because over the past couple of years, a lot of developers have gone bust or shrunk down, leaving a landscape that's barren of resources. It's like a big venerable tree has collapsed in the forest. There's now this giant space, where light falls on the woodland ground, where not much light used to fall. In this space, in the natural world, saplings and undergrowth burst into life and eventually it's likely a new tree will win out over their competitors and become the next venerable one to stand proud and tall and dominate the space. It's exactly the same in business: small start-ups are beginning to fill up as the business landscape has changed and allowed them to do things like Xbox Live Arcade, Sony Marketplace, or whatever new subscription service is successful. But in terms of the medium-sized guys like us, it seems like they've either died off or had to get bigger. Similarly, what we've heard anecdotally is a lot of the big publishers think there are only between ten and twenty developers in the world who can do big, high quality nextgen games. This means the publishers are competing to find games from an ever smaller resource of talented games makers.

After the success of *World of Warcraft* there was a huge rush to make MMOs, Massively Multiplayer Online games. Billions of dollars went into that market – and billions of dollars were made, but even the biggest successes have a decline. It used to be the eighty–twenty rule: eighty percent of games don't have much success, twenty percent do. I think that's oversimplified these days and of course making enough from a game to keep going is fine. The trick to success, is, of course, to be able to tell which title falls into which category. I was once told by a senior executive of a company that does not now exist that not all of their games were successful so they only marketed about twenty percent of them, and surprisingly enough about that number were successful. I did point out that if there was a strong correlation between sales success and actual marketing effort, they might want to reconsider their strategy, but the point went over the executive's head. He wasn't very bright, but he did have a lot of family contacts in the City of London investment circles. This is another aspect of prudence: don't be blinded by the bullshit, or at least know it's bullshit and use that to your advantage when investing. There's a significant number of companies in what is euphemistically called the 'pre-profit' stage of their growth that are highly valued by the public markets. They haven't actually ever made any money at all and have no clear route to do so, and arguably as long as they can delay the need to make a profit they can continue to sell the sizzle. The US model is, ironically, built on failure. Fail fast, fail often, spin to the next one. Everyone seems to want to make £1,000 from £100 rather than £110 from £100. Stocks and shares are therefore largely a form of abstracted gambling rather than based on anything vaguely concrete: you have something someone else wants, and you hold onto it because you think it will go up in value. It's like a racehorse trainer constantly telling you how good a particular horse is but never actually letting it run.

People are so desperate to be ahead of the game that some of them'll believe almost anything, they just want to believe and any evidence against that desire is ignored or reduced in importance or excused. It seems that the human brain is wired to think like this sometimes. There was a Miami-based company called Magic Leap which promised amazing augmented reality (AR) headsets and secured something like $4 billion in funding. Of course, what they promised was both out-of-this-world and suitably vague all at the same time: 'The technology is amazingly ground-breaking, but also understand that we can't reveal details right now.' They got celebrities to invest which helped promote it, showed tech demos in carefully controlled circumstances, which were awesome according to some of the lucky few who were allowed to see it, which all added to the frenzy of investment, and everyone piled in. But all they had to sell initially was a tech demo and the sizzle: when it eventually launched, reality bit down hard and the market was unimpressed. Before that was something called Project Ginger that was going to 'change the way cities work'; again, celebrities and investors got involved mostly, it appears, on the basis of the sizzle. It turned out to be the definitely innovative Segway. A fun niche vehicle, with some interesting tech that, according to some commentators is much less useful than a bicycle really. Did it change cities? Not even slightly. Is it a fun product? Yes.

Selling something from behind the glittery green curtain is not a new thing, of course. Carnival sideshows have been selling the promise of something extraordinary inside for centuries, and some of the audience falls for it every time. Some of them may even find seeing the incredible fish boy worth their penny, but many are disappointed. We're all curious monkeys at heart. What's on offer behind the canvas wall may change as technology advances, but human nature remains the same. It's 180 years since Charles Mackay wrote his seminal work *Extraordinary Popular Delusions and the Madness of Crowds*, and the newspapers of his day were full of scams – 'Send £5 to this address for unprecedented opportunities', that kind of thing. Some of them are even semi-honest, though not what people expected. I remember a small ad at the back of some newspapers that said, 'Send £5 and I'll give you instructions on how to earn hundreds of pounds easily.' What turned up, if you sent off your money, was a simple page of instructions to place small ads asking for £5 to get exactly this advice and place your own small ads. It's honest, I suppose, but deceptive, and I'm not sure if it's illegal or not. So much of economic theory is based on the assumption of rational operators, but that's a big (and to my mind provably unjustified) assumption. Some people, a very few, are mostly rational all the time, the rest might be rational some of the time depending on their quirks, but there are still others who seem to be wholly irrational most of the time. Economic theory works best when people are rational, though it'd probably be almost impossible to manage theories when people act irrationally, but it also might be a fun research project and field of study.

Take *Words With Friends*, which also used the power of celebrities on social media to promote themselves into a big media phenomenon. They had three suitors and made a fortune, selling the whole company just before the market turned, and fortunes waned as fast as they had waxed. Moshi Monsters, for example, did very well but were found to have broken the rules in their advertising (the ASA hauled them over the coals for encouraging pester power) and their business stumbled after finally being forced to change and follow the rules like everyone else. In effect, one of the reasons for their rapid success was that they hadn't been following the rules that everyone else had been following, so had a major advantage. That's not being a business executive. That's being a carnival barker. It's like that old adage about politicians campaigning in poetry and governing in prose: well, managing business is prose. The latest whizz-bang stock that's all the rage might be superficially sexy, but investing mostly in unsexy stuff is often a less risky bet.

Money, itself, is an abstraction of value, and it has been further abstracted in many people's minds in the digital revolution. Part of prudence is always remembering how real it is. How hard to gather, and how easy to spend. I never forget the early days of Rebellion, when just getting invoices paid on time was a challenge every month and there was a lot of stress around collecting invoices that may have been small for a client but were almost life or death for us. Good interpersonal skills were essential, and keeping an eye on cash flow is one of the important things that you have to do in any business. You also need to keep an eye on why you're not getting paid; maybe they're having money troubles themselves. Knowing that early can help decide your tactics going forward.

This personal and very physical reality of money echoes back to medieval times, when they used tally sticks to prove both halves of a bargain. A tally stick was a single stick with notches of various sizes carved into one or more edges to record data. Many of them also had writing that crossed the divide, as the initially single stick was split lengthways, with each half having part of the carving on it. Subsequently this could be physically matched together to prove a payment. It also usually had a long and a short part. The long was the stock (you probably recognise that from its use in the stock market), the short was the foil or counterfoil, and this use of tally sticks in one form or another lasted till 1837 – that is, 600 years of financial records being kept on cut sticks. The counterfoil nomenclature is, of course, still used in banking to this day. Tally sticks were a form of data encryption and physical blockchain, just hand carved into wood, carbon neutral and long-lasting, requiring no energy-guzzling computers anywhere, just a shelf somewhere safe. And the word 'stock', well that comes from several northern European languages and is just the word for stick, so in very real terms, the modern stock market is the stick market, in which ownership of something intangible, like shares in a business, are encoded on cut sticks. Richard FitzNeal's 12th-century *Dialogue of the Exchequer* describes a tally as, 'The distance between the tip of the forefinger and the thumb when fully extended. The manner of cutting is as follows. At the top of the tally a cut is made, the thickness of the palm of the hand, to represent £1,000; then £100 by a cut the breadth of a thumb; £20, the breadth of the little finger; a single pound, the width of a swollen barleycorn; a shilling rather narrower than a penny is marked by a single cut without removing any wood.'

Tally sticks were more or less the first artefact of thought and memory, and have been around for thousands and thousands of years: the first animal bones carved with notches came during the Upper Palaeolithic age around 45,000 years ago, and they have been mentioned by such historical notables as Pliny the Elder and Marco Polo. The earliest notched bones we have seem to record twenty-eight of something and it's been suggested that this might be a record of an early human woman's recording of her monthly cycle. In medieval times they morphed from being single sticks to split sticks, so party and counterparty could have a matching duplicate: there was a constant shortage of coins and many people were illiterate, and people could pay a scribe to write anything. In typical physical practical style so beloved of the medieval era, notches were made on a stick to record the amount in question and then the stick was split lengthwise and each party received one half. Sticks being sticks, with their own unique wood grain pattern, and their own features, only the original halves would fit with each other perfectly. Counterfeiting would have been very difficult indeed, meaning there was little chance of mistaken identity, accounting errors or attempts to alter the amount in question after the fact. The system worked so well that it was not only accepted as legal proof in medieval courts: it was mentioned in the Napoleonic Code of 1804, and in rural parts of Switzerland it was still being used in the 20th century. In England, Parliament decided to burn all the tally sticks in 1834 – they had fallen out of favour by then – but the resultant fire spiralled out of control and burned down pretty much the entire Palace of Westminster. What millions of tourists visit today is what was built to replace it after the fire was brought under control. Only the great hall, now called simply Westminster Hall (built in the reign of the son of William the Conqueror, William Rufus, in 1097), remained mostly intact. Perhaps it was some form of divine justice held over from medieval times or the revenge of the working classes against their noble bosses? Most likely it was too many very dry sticks burned in one place at the same time by workmen in a rush. All that recorded history going up in smoke to save some storage space. I hope someone was horribly ashamed of making that decision.

What I really like about this system was that it treated money not as something impersonal and neutral but as a marker of a bilateral agreement between two parties, with all the concomitant issues of trust and mutual reliance. It was in essence a local system, because people didn't easily go far from home too often in those days, and so people knew each other; they probably knew who would honour their debts and who wouldn't. Of course, the system inevitably became more complex, with tally sticks gradually coming to be used both as their own secondary markets and as guarantees of government debt, but I still like to think of it as an act of trust between two people.

Beyond that, you get into irrationality and sentiment. There is nothing rational, for example, about the use of gold as the *ne plus ultra* of currency value, other than the fact that it's long been that way, it's relatively rare and hard to fake: its continued use is reliant on everyone continuing to buy into it as a concept, and its value is therefore partly a social construct. It's by no means a useless metal – it's ductile so can be hammered very thinly, it doesn't tarnish, and so on – but it's mainly its history and comparative rarity which makes it so valuable, at least in terms of investment value (the gold bars in the vaults of the Bank of England or the Federal Reserve aren't being used in any functional way). It's also beautiful, lustrous, warm and shiny, which sparks emotional responses in people.

But if astronomers were to discover a 100 million tonne asteroid made of gold and bring it back to earth then gold might become worthless. The conquistador Hernan Cortes and his men were obsessed with all the gold jewellery and ornaments they found in the Aztec capital Tenochtitlan, but for the Aztecs, who had plenty of gold, these were commonplace and they found the Spaniards' attitudes puzzling (something also alluded to in Thomas More's *Utopia*, where the Utopians use gold for everything and therefore mistake visiting ambassadors laden with the stuff for menial servants). The coronation crown of Frederick I, Holy Roman Emperor, featured a dome of purest aluminium accented and encrusted with diamonds and gold, but it was the aluminium which was the rarest and most valuable of those three at the time (it wasn't until electricity came along and made smelting easier that aluminium became commonplace. There's about one hundred soft drink cans' worth in the dome). Even today, there are plenty of metals more expensive, rarer and arguably more useful than gold.

Prudence also involves working through cognitive fallacies and false positives. Just because someone made a good decision once doesn't mean they'll always be right; just because someone was successful on one occasion doesn't mean that their reasoning or actions were flawless; just because someone got something wrong doesn't mean their fundamentals weren't sound. A friend of mine cashed out of the first dot com boom in early 2000, thinking the bubble had to burst sometime soon. But the stocks kept on rising, and a few months later, when he went on holiday, he resolved to buy back into the market the moment he returned to the office. Of course, the market crashed while he was still abroad and he was hailed as this great prophetic genius! He got lucky, and was the first to admit it (well, to a few of us, anyway...).

It's fascinating and a privilege to live through times like this, not least because they demonstrate over and again the futility of trying to be right the whole time. An in-depth examination of any historical episode will show that those making the decisions were wrong almost as much as they were right, not because they were stupid or venal but because they were dealing with events cascading on a vast scale and across myriad arenas, and those events by definition unfolded at least partially in ways which could not reasonably have been foreseen. Good decisions are only educated guesses, after all, and getting five percent more than random chance correct is very good going in a chaotic world, especially when you consider the cumulative effect of that compound interest piling up. One of the things I believe taught in officer training is the need to make a decision, any decision, then have more of your decisions be right rather than wrong. Making an actual decision is the first step and is hard for many people.

The ability to foresee things, or predict the outcome of something marginally better than random chance, is a priceless one, precisely because it's so difficult. The movie *Margin Call* takes place over one night in an investment bank facing ruin, and in the movie's pivotal scene the CEO John Tuld (played by Jeremy Irons) tells a meeting of all his senior people, 'Do you care to know why I'm in this chair with you all? I mean, why I earn the big bucks? I'm here for one reason and one reason alone. I'm here to guess what the music might do a week, a month, a year from now. That's it. Nothing more.'

It is a depressingly accurate line as far as Wall Street is concerned, but also a depressingly cynical one. Money is one of the things you need to make projects happen, a necessary fuel that can be used wisely or foolishly, but it isn't an end in itself as far as I'm concerned. Lack of money can mean more difficulty and stress of course, though there are plenty of people without much money who are happy, just as there are many people with a lot of money who are miserable. The joke being that money buys you a better quality of misery.

I remember the point at which we had over £1 million in the bank, actual money to be spent on projects and exciting things. My brother came in and told me, six years into the business. We shook hands and congratulated each other in an understated British way, then got on with the rest of the day. Whilst it was a fun moment, significant numbers are really just the next number after the less significant one; they resonate with the pattern recognition part of our human brains that I've discussed earlier. Numerology is all about seeing patterns in numbers where there are no patterns, and maths is about finding patterns where there are actual patterns. There was no need to slow down. A business is something that constantly flows, exactly like a river. If you really think about what a river is, is it a space where water flows past, or is the water itself the river, or is the river the concept of constant motion of water?

On a personal note, I try to keep spending and saving in balance, but I'm probably more a saver overall. I spend when I think there is something worth spending money on, and try to buy quality, so spending a little more rather than buying cheaply and buying twice, an aphorism taught to me by my maternal granny. For me life is mostly about experiences and doing things, not having things (with a few notable exceptions like horses, swords and suits of armour). I want to keep the business going well, making games, books and comics for others to enjoy. I also want to teach people about history, help people learn how to run an ethical business, and do more research into how horses have been trained in the past.

There's nothing I dream about purchasing. I don't want a fast car or a yacht, and I've never understood having lots of houses around the world. If you want to go on holiday and you've got that much money, just take a hotel suite or a villa for as long as you need. I like to have roots. I've got more than enough horses, and in any case I can only ride one of them at a time (unless I'm trick riding). I don't want to get complacent. If I buy a new sword and it's made by a specialist sword maker I want to appreciate it, and use it too. I'm a big believer in using things you have. My armour is dented and in used condition, as it should be.

I took out a small pension at eighteen. I worked out the

maths and thought the earlier I started the better. Now I think of my pension as a safety net, but I have plenty of other plans to create future income. Horses are a wasting asset unless they are breeding stallions or mares of course. Physical property is important to me. I bought my farm of around 165 acres in 2006. One shouldn't necessarily rely on all one's wealth to be managed and recorded by computers. I don't believe in complete reliance on potentially brittle systems. My ideal is to spread money across investments, property, things that matter to me, and upgrading my own skills, hence why I'm learning the practicalities of farming and growing food. Not to be too much of a medieval survivalist, but it can never hurt to be as self-reliant as possible, and growing and harvesting some of your own food is fun and helps you really appreciate the turning of the seasons. Currently I always seem to miss the early planting season for fear of late frosts, but my potato harvests have been fairly good and I'm learning by doing, failing and doing again.

I think having too much money can potentially become a burden, as odd as that sounds to almost all of us. Money, acquisitions, awards: these sorts of things actually are gamifications; they motivate people, but it's not always healthy. The three richest men in America – Elon Musk, Jeff Bezos and Bill Gates – are between them worth more than the poorest half of America, totalling 160 million people in all. You don't have to be a card-carrying member of the Communist Party to think that that is very odd and probably not, on balance, a good or healthy thing for society overall. Literally nobody can work hard enough to be a billionaire: to be worth that much money involves doing something separate from hard work. It involves owning shares in something that lots of other people want to buy and sell parts of, or building something from modest roots into a massive organisation through recognising that you're in the right place at the right time with the right idea, but also skill, determination, and almost always a decent amount of luck too. When you're that rich, the concept of money must cease to mean anything: there's very little you can't buy. I'd argue that happiness is one of the things you really can't buy, same as true friendship, love and respect. That comes from human relationships, and some relationships can be purchased, but not many, and not the really important ones. Instead wealth becomes a proxy for power and access; in effect it's points on a scale, a high score on the videogame display of life. How many people, including – especially – world leaders wouldn't take a call from any of those people? You should get a certificate once you have a certain amount of money: good, well done, you've won this part of the game, but now the rules have changed and you have to go forward and do some decent things for other people's lives. Somebody worked out that Smaug, the dragon in Tolkien's *The Hobbit*, sat on a gold horde of vast size. He was a greedy monster with vast appetites for wealth, but would only rank in about twentieth place in the list of the richest humans.

You often hear it said that someone has the Midas touch, and that everything they touch turns to gold, but people forget that the story of Midas was a warning rather than an encomium: that there are only so many things one can do with money after all. The Latin poet Claudian said in his *In Rufinum*: 'So Midas, king of Lydia, swelled at first with pride when he found he could transform everything he touched to gold; but when he beheld his food grow rigid and his drink harden into golden ice then he understood that this gift was a bane and in his loathing for gold, cursed his prayer.' As an aside I've always wondered what the rules of Midas's power would be. Does he have to touch something with his skin to make the transformation happen, could he manage with gloves, which would of course become gold and stiffen up, would his power work through more gold? Gold things are a lot heavier than most non-gold things, so a table might collapse under the curse. Could he turn a whole palace into gold, or would he have to touch each stone in turn? What about a river? Would the water that flowed past him turn to gold? What's the goldification range of this power? He'd likely die of starvation or severe gastric issues very quickly as the food inside him turned to gold. (Technically our guts are still 'outside' our bodies, as we're topologically big biological doughnuts.) Nasty. Sometimes a game designer's mind is a fun place. Along with the tale of King Canute, Midas is perhaps the most misunderstood myth out there. Canute's futile attempts to turn back the tide were deliberate, they were not a sign of his arrogance or hubris: rather, they were his attempts to show his courtiers the extent of his kingly powers, and the things he could not do rather than the ones he could. It was all about the limits of earthly power.

The example of Charles Webb is perhaps an extreme one, but it shows how it is possible to think against the conventional grain. Webb wrote the 1963 novel *The Graduate*, which of course became a hit film four years later. He received only $20,000 for the rights and refused an additional $10,000 offered by the film's producer once it had made millions. Originally from a well-off family, he turned down his inheritance and donated his royalties to charity. He, his wife Eve and their sons lived cheaply, for a time in a camper van. 'My wife and I have done a lot of things we wouldn't have done if we were rich people. I would have been counting my money instead of educating my children,' he said. 'We just felt more comfortable living a fairly basic lifestyle. When you run out of money it's a purifying experience. It focuses the mind like nothing else.

You sometimes regret not being the kind of person who sorts out savings bonds or insurance policies. But you reach a point when you have flashes of insight into things. If I'd had $100 million it wouldn't have taken me that much longer to spend than $20,000.'

That level of insight and honesty is rare. In Cannes harbour once I went to a party on a yacht. I didn't know the owner from Adam, but a friend of a friend was going so I tagged along; the food and wine was very welcome to me, an impoverished student living temporarily in a very damp, but equally cheap, bedsit. The next day, this self-same yacht had all its shutters down and there was no sign of life on board. It turned out that overnight a bigger yacht had arrived in harbour, and the owner of the yacht I'd been on couldn't cope with this. If he was the biggest fish in the pond (or rather the harbour) he was happy to entertain total strangers such as me, but if he wasn't he wouldn't even come out. He had more money than he could spend in dozens of lifetimes and more things than most people have ever had, but he couldn't cope with being number two.

That's not competitiveness: that's a mental error, a ranking of someone's worth by all the things that are unimportant and none of the things that are important. Unless you are the single richest human, there will always be someone richer. That richest person in turn will not be the best athlete, who in turn will not be considered the best looking, so you might always be driven to try to take the next step up, heedless of the fact that none of those steps will give you satisfaction unless and until you accept that any of the steps could give you satisfaction if only you'd allow them to. You are what you measure, and I've always tried to measure the right things. The fastest runner is unlikely to be the best at chess, or the greatest golfer, good at plumbing. Nobody is the best at everything. Some people are very good at a lot of things, some the best at a few. There are certainly many who are pretty average at most things but are very happy. Sometimes to try to become the best at something means that by necessity you must make sacrifices and get worse at others or miss out on important things. When looking at successful professional sports people I wonder how many people never even tried that particular sport, and so just don't know that they might have been the best at it? Some sports are quite obscure, or even require expensive equipment to compete. How many people from Africa might be great ice hockey players, but never think about trying it? Equestrian sports need a lot of money to buy, train and maintain a set of competitive horses (most competitive people have several horses at various stages of training). How many people never get to try riding and find out if they might have an aptitude for it?

Chapter Six

Temperance

TEMPERANCE IS ANOTHER word which over the years has taken on certain connotations: in this case, earnest men and women speaking in hushed tones of the evil of alcohol and the need to spurn it at every turn. As someone who drinks only very occasionally – not through any conviction that the nearest can of beer is the devil's buttermilk, but as a matter of personal choice – I have no real skin in this particular game. Instead, I think of temperance as being something broader and more holistic: an application of moderation across the board and a tenet by which various parts of my life can be kept in balance.

First, the application of moderation. This involves voluntary self-restraint in several areas: restraint from revenge by practising non-violence and forgiveness, restraint from arrogance by practising humility and modesty, and restraint from excesses by refusing to indulge in extravagant luxury. In essence, it involves restraining an excess of an impulse. The Latin word *tempero* means just this, restraint, but it also means a moderate method of government or control and proper balancing or mixing. A medieval sword was hardened and tempered when it was forged through skilful heating and cooling. To my mind temperance is about getting the balance right, it doesn't go as far as ascetic self-denial, as that might be considered immodest, nor does it allow gluttonous indulgence, but a sensible middle ground between those two extremes. There is quite a range of options between the two end points.

As discussed in the previous chapter, I'm not flash with my money, I'm not deliberately 'not flash' if you see what I mean, and I don't live like an anchorite monk. Aside from more horses than is sensible, I've amassed a fair amount of original artwork from comics. That's recently become very collectable and valuable. I have occasionally indulged in business or even first-class flights if I'm travelling for work (though in the last few years I have hardly flown anywhere unless it's essential I do so), mostly because that means I can work on the flight, get some fair sleep and get to meetings in good spirits. But otherwise I like to have a reasonably frugal mindset, and always have. Chris and I didn't raise cash when we started Rebellion. We used our modest savings and didn't take out any personal wages for ages. Our business was based at home, so the morning commute was to fling open windows to get some fresh air in and walk around the block, just to have a change of scenery. It was very exciting and energising, and that was enough for us.

The adventure books I wrote aged eighteen featured a world where black and white were evil and shades of colour were good. It was a deliberate choice, and I only realised it a bit later, but when I did I knew instantly where it had come from: my heartfelt distrust of extremism in any form. I don't indulge extremists or lunatics on any far end of the political web, and my politics don't sit neatly into one or other position. All life is generally about nuance and balance. Not every correct answer is in between two extremes of course, it's perfectly possible for one side to be wrong and the other correct, and there is this odd creeping concept that balance in the media is to be found in having someone with nutty views to 'balance' the sensible, fact-based reasonable person's views. That's just wrong. However, there are very few questions of significance worth asking to which the answer is both easy and simple.

Managing excess is always a good thing. In medieval times it was occasionally the job of the church to manage the excesses of absolute monarchs. Where a king had one crown and an emperor two, the pope wore three: a constant reminder that, though the first two could (and did) claim their divine rights to rule, only the last spoke for God. In this way the behaviour of monarchs was supposedly moderated, to varying degrees of success of course, because the ultimate punishment, excommunication, was a casting out from the church and therefore suggesting the abusive monarch would face Judgement Day as an apostate. This was the ultimate card the church could play and seems to have been used as a threat quite successfully for a long time. Perhaps kings were more worried about their subjects' opinions and behaviour rather than their personal post-death issues. This went on for centuries until the science and reason and the rise of Protestantism began to chip away at it and disconnect people from that network.

Second, balance between work and life. Tarot cards also date from the late Middle Ages, and Temperance (card XIV in the traditional major arcana) also reflects the importance of balance. The angel on the card is both masculine and feminine, it has one foot on land and the other in water, and it is mixing water between two cups. Everything about this card represents the harmony which comes from keeping dualities in equilibrium.

I like working, doing productive things. There aren't many other things I'd like to be doing, but if I wasn't doing this then one of the jobs I'd consider would be a stuntman. Seriously. I think they have an interesting and challenging life and I have a lot of appreciation for the craft skills that they use on set and their patience working with actors who are maybe not as physically controlled as may be ideal. As it is, I have had a great working life. Some energising ups and draining downs, some easy decisions, some very hard ones, mostly great, creative and talented colleagues. Every single project I work on is a favourite at some stage or another. Just the very act of getting a project started then finished and out there in public and having people play it is a fantastic and difficult thing to do. Many game developers fail to get their game finished. Estimates vary but some people suggest only about a third of games ever get finished and released, of the few that are even started. I don't have a single favourite game I've ever worked on – I think every single one of them, even the ones that didn't quite work out the way we wanted them to, are among my favourites. Having said that, some titles mark significant points in our history; so the first game I ever designed was bizarrely a 'parody shooter' (a sub-genre of game that has not really caught on) called *Better Dead Than Alien*. My first 'big' game was also very innovative for the time. It was heavily influenced by medieval myths and shadow puppets and was called *Blade Warrior*. It had full screen graphics and differential scrolling of screen elements to give depth. More recently I suppose *Alien vs. Predator* and then *Sniper Elite* are hugely important game milestones for Rebellion and us personally, but all the games we do mark significant moments.

Jason Kingsley

So for me the 'balance' in work-life balance works both ways.
It's not simply getting away with as little work as possible: it's a
matter of finding the point at which both sides of the equation
play off each other, with your work informing your passions
and your passions informing your work. At the moment I'm
eighty percent work and twenty percent horses, but I could
imagine a time when it might be 50:50. Humans are much
like horses. If you get put out to pasture, you often mope and
fade away. A horse tends to live a lot longer if it does a modest
amount of work.

People ask whether we work to live or live to work. My
answer is it should be both, if you're doing it right. It's not a
simple equation that work provides money and money buys
what we need to live: it's more complex and holistic than that. I
don't necessarily think of work and leisure as separate entities,
though many people do. I enjoy business, I have seventeen
horses to look after and an active farm so theoretically
managing my farm is a full-time job, but I never see any of the
variety of hats I have to wear as anything other than things I
want to do. People ask how I switch off, and the short answer
is that I don't. I switch *over*.

While I'm handling or training horses I think about nothing
else as it's so consuming. A young horse can be unpredictable
and if upset can panic. A panicking 400-kilogramme package
of muscle and very little brain hurts a lot when it crashes into
you. You need to stay aware and switched on, especially with
youngsters. I can slightly switch off when out riding across the
landscape, on the more experienced horses, and let my mind
wander, but even then there's a base level of concentration
which needs to be maintained. Riding and controlling a horse
is something I am able to do subconsciously to a large extent.
I've been riding that long that when instructing someone, I

have to think the movement then translate it into words. When you are training a horse at advanced level what you're really doing is having a two-way communication, a discussion. I'm really bad at going on holiday: I just can't do it, I can't lie down and do nothing. I have really tried, and failed many times. I have on several occasions decided to go home early as I was getting bored and frustrated and just not enjoying the time, even counting down the days until my return journey. I don't even like going to restaurants usually (though I have been to some amazing ones and I fully appreciate the craft and service skills that go into them). People seem to spend a lot of time in them, achieving very little (and being waited on makes me feel a bit odd). But these are very personal things and I'm well aware that lots of people don't feel that way. I certainly don't think restaurants are a bad thing, they're just not really my thing very often.

That doesn't alter the central point about balance: it's not about what you do, but how much time and effort you give to each thing in your life. If one thing is becoming disproportionately time-consuming or feels like too much effort, then things are out of whack. If your hobby feels like a badly paid job, you need to make some changes. It doesn't matter what that thing is: it matters how much of your life it absorbs. It's easy to get too bunged up about work, but perfectionism is the enemy of both reality and happiness. I don't doubt that I've probably lost a few deals as a result of being seen as eccentric, frivolous or stupid. But the older you get the faster you realise how important it is for all of us to do as many of the things that make us feel as happy as we can, even if that's looking out of the window at the falling rain.

I don't want to burn out or see people I work with burn out. Not only does that make us less productive in the long run,

"There aren't many successful chief executives who can be seen on the internet swinging an axe at a watermelon."

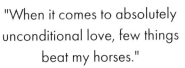

"When it comes to absolutely unconditional love, few things beat my horses."

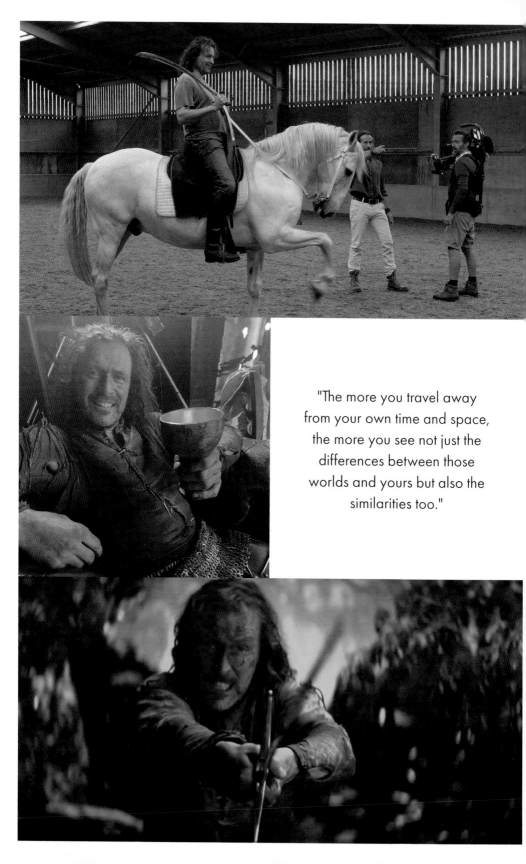

"The more you travel away from your own time and space, the more you see not just the differences between those worlds and yours but also the similarities too."

"This is why I love medieval horsemanship and riding through the English countryside. It's a form of escape, adventure and even time travel."

"I love exploring the frontier of technology, which combined with entertainment is always an exciting area. For me at Rebellion, my faith is that we are in our own small way making the world a better place."

but much more importantly it damages mental and physical health too. Overworking raises the risk of anxiety, depression, sleep deprivation, strokes and heart attacks, let alone the effect it can have on relationships. On a purely business level, no company should want unhappy staff (with the single exception of funeral workers I suppose, though they only need to look unhappy superficially). Unhappy staff eventually means a high staff turnover, and it costs money to hire new people and time to train them up, but really the issue is that I prefer to work with happy, engaged and skilful co-workers. It makes my job so much easier. But on a broader level, I don't want anyone who works for me to regard their job as a thing they have to withstand. Ideally I want them to walk into the job each day with a genuine spring in their step and a positive outlook, but that comes only if they're both energised and rested. I realise that's probably unrealistic for everyone all the time, but hopefully it's possible for most of the team, most of the time. It's a two-way relationship between employer and employee, and must always be. Even when I interview someone, I don't want to be the only one thinking, 'Is this going to be a good fit?' A company has to be right for an employee quite as much as vice versa. It's awful when someone is asked in an interview why they want to work here, and their answer is that they 'just need a job'. I know it's true, and it also shows honesty, but I'd prefer the answer to be 'I really want to make games', or something similar.

So I try to talk to staff and ask for their feedback. Often I don't get it unless someone is very unhappy, which is a shame as often senior management sometimes feels a bit like crisis management. Problems only get up to our level if they're severe and big. I'm told that junior and mid-level staff feel intimidated by the big bosses, and don't want to speak to us directly, or are put off doing so because we're so busy. This is covered more fully in Chapter Eight, 'Truth', but for now it's enough to say that any kind of balance by its nature involves a balance of information flow too. There isn't much point me laying down dictates about working hours and the like if what's needed is something totally different, and the people who will know that are the people who are being affected. What changes do they think would improve their situation?

We try not to ask for too much overtime from our teams, it's usually voluntary as some people have complex home lives and dependants who need their attention, and it's almost always only needed at the very end of a project when we're trying to get the best, most polished game out there and the release deadline is looming. I know the games development industry has a chequered reputation for demanding over-work and terms like 'crunch' and the even more difficult 'death march' are part of the zeitgeist of making games. Neither should really be either necessary or desirable in a well-managed games-making process. Finding the balance for some people can be especially hard in creative professions, where the criteria for success or quality can be more nebulous and subjective. If everyone hated their jobs, it would be much easier to create work-life balance. Employees feel a sense of competition with each other, and one of the ways in which this competitiveness can manifest itself is in trying to outwork each other. Work-life balance only changes when those in power choose to do something about it, make changes happen: employees, in normal circumstances, are rarely going to remould a workplace culture off their own bat, certainly not in situations of moderate mismanagement. We do have examples of very extreme direct action taken by workers historically of course, from the peasants' revolt of medieval England to the more recent armed revolutions. If they have to resort to collective action to do so, then I would suggest that as a boss you have failed badly by letting it get to that point, and if they've gone as far as collecting guns or pitchforks, then absolutely your management style needs changing!

It's all very well saying that you want to achieve a work/life balance, but putting into practice the measures needed to achieve that is a different matter entirely. In particular, we need to unpick the mindset which equates long working hours with productivity and success. Yes, there are times when a project is nearing completion and people do need to work extra hours, but those times should be few and far between and voluntary. For the vast majority of the time, a manageable amount of working hours is not just achievable but actively desirable. American academic Matt Might describes 'the equation of work' as 'output = unit of work / hour × hours worked'. Neither part works without the other. I want my people to work smarter rather than longer.

This 'I need to work long hours' mindset is a pernicious one, and has been around a long time. It may have started in investment banks – it's certainly most associated with them – and apart from all the obvious reasons to dislike it, it has always struck me as more than a bit performative. I think that a lot of it is the desire to be seen as working hard rather than the need for hard work itself: impress the boss, make yourself seem industrious, invaluable and irreplaceable, and so on. I'm not interested in performative shows of hard work: I'm interested in people working sensibly and doing their jobs properly. Sensibly might mean different things for different people and even different things for the same person at certain stages of their life. If people are regularly having to work insane hours, then not only is something wrong, but that something is my fault. Either they have too much work, in which case I have to employ more people or scale back their workload, or they have a normal amount of work but aren't competent enough to get through it in time, in which case I need to move them to a less demanding job or give them training.

I try to get people to ignore the damaging 'shoulds', whether they're external or internal. The external ones are what other people tell you that you should be doing, and the internal ones are what you tell yourself you should be doing, themselves distilled from social and workplace attitudes which you've collected over the years. The shift in attitudes towards work is a generational thing, with millennials more likely than their elders to blur the lines between work and home: but in terms of work/life balance this doesn't have to be an altogether bad thing, if in blurring these lines they also want to choose when to work and how best to use their time (video meetings rather than real ones).

The balance and divide I want to see isn't a geographical or physical one: it's a mental one, as is the need for the switch between life aspects. Balance is not simply about allocating a certain amount of hours each day to various tasks – work, family time, exercise, meals, social life etc. It's about ensuring that you switch off – or rather switch over – between those various aspects when it's time to do so. There's no point saying that you spend x hours a week away from work if you're still taking that work home with you mentally: thinking about it, stressing about it, answering e-mails. You haven't switched over totally, and though you may be physically present wherever you are, mentally and emotionally you're not.

So I try to practise what I preach. I can't tell people not to be working late at night if I'm sending them e-mails at two in the morning or staying in the office long after dark. I don't expect my employees to answer e-mails outside work hours, unless it's very urgent or an emergency. The ubiquity of technology, and the fact that everyone has a smartphone and wifi now, means that the whole 'I'm out of contact' autoreply carries ever less weight. It's unfair to put the burden of a quick reply onto the recipient. If you make it clear that you don't expect an answer till office hours, then they feel much less pressured to break into their leisure time. And holiday allowance is there for a reason. When I say that I don't go on holiday, what I mean is that I don't go and lie on a beach.

I'm aware that our industry is not altogether representative of society: it's a fairly male-dominated one, both in terms of those who work in it and those who consume our products, and therefore we have far fewer mothers in our workforce, and mothers still tend to bear the brunt of trying to balance a hectic home life with a productive work one (individual circumstances may be at variance with this of course). But even so: for everyone it can sometimes seem that achieving a work/life balance is almost an act of subversion or resistance, and that's not right.

One of the best ways of seeing how imbalance can be counterproductive is through the parable of the Mexican fisherman and the American banker. An American investment banker was on holiday in a Mexican fishing village when a small boat docked. Aboard was a single fisherman with his catch of yellowfin tuna.

'They're some great-looking fish,' the banker said. 'How long did it take to catch them?'

'Oh, not long,' the fisherman said. 'A couple of hours, no more.'

'Then why don't you stay out longer? Imagine how many fish you could catch if you stayed out all day.'

'I catch enough to feed my family. That's what matters.'

'But what do you do with the rest of your time?'

'I sleep late, play with my children, have lunch, take a siesta with my wife, and every evening I stroll into the village where I sip wine and play guitar with my amigos.'

'That's it?'

'That's it.'

'Listen. I'm an Ivy League MBA, and I can help you.'

'How?'

'Instead of spending two hours a day fishing, you spend eight hours a day. You catch four times as many fish as you do now and you sell the excess. With the money from that you buy a bigger boat and get to bring back an even bigger catch. With the money from that you buy several more boats and employ people to go out in them. You pay them a wage but keep the proceeds from the catch. Soon you have a whole fleet of fishing boats, so instead of selling your catch to the middleman you sell directly to the processor. Eventually you make so much money that you buy out the cannery, and now you control the product, processing and distribution.'

'This village is too small for all that.'

'Of course. You'd need to move to Mexico City to run this empire, and maybe after that even New York.'

'But señor, how long will this all take?'

'Fifteen years, probably. Maybe twenty.'

'And then?'

'This is the best part. You announce an IPO, take your company public, and become rich. Very rich. Tens of millions rich.'

'Then what?'

'Then you retire. You move to a small fishing village where you sleep late, play with your grandchildren, have lunch, take a siesta with your wife, and every evening you stroll into the village where you sip wine and play guitar with your amigos.'

Chapter Seven

Resolution

THE WORD 'RESOLUTION' has several different meanings, all of which are applicable in one way or another to running a business. There's resolution as in resolve and resilience, resolution as in making a decision or solving a problem, resolution as in a promise to oneself, and resolution as in the level of visible detail. They all come back to the same thing: leadership, which in turn can be broken down into constituent parts spelling out the word 'resolution' itself.

Resilience. Resilience and perseverance are important. 'Do not judge me by my success,' said Nelson Mandela. 'Judge me by how many times I fell down and got back up again.' Everything always takes a lot longer to happen than you thought it would, and you'd never start it if you knew how long it would take. Starting a business is one of the hardest parts of being in business.

Anyone can have an idea, but it's a long way from that to getting off your arse, having a go and doing something about it. So many businesses fold before they're even started. Lots fail afterwards, and the first three years are particularly difficult. Just staying in business is an achievement worth congratulating yourself for.

Making the first thousand is harder than making the first million; that's not to say there won't be a lot of ups and downs on the way to that second landmark, and indeed beyond it. No progress is ever linear, whatever spreadsheets might try to tell you, and whatever business plan you concoct. The important thing about both the troughs and peaks is that neither last. Therefore every leader needs to be able to take the rough with the smooth, because there'll be as much of one as the other, and to keep a sense of perspective whatever the situation. Anyone can be a leader when things are going well: fewer people can lead when things are going against them. I generally feel that one or two things going wrong at the same time is quite manageable, three to four is a bit more difficult, but five or more needs specific prioritisation of what to fix first. Weirdly (and this is probably as much about how human minds work as anything real statistically), bad things do seem to arrive in threes more often that you might expect. Resilience is not freedom from or the absence of failure, pain or distress: it's experiencing those things and going through them to the other side. Picking yourself up after being knocked back or down. In many ways what goes wrong teaches us more than what goes right. There's no resilience needed to travel down a smooth road really, apart from the willingness to actually travel in the first place. Maybe Winston Churchill said it best, and most simply, of all: 'When you're going through hell, keep going.' What he said and what he did are often at odds though, so listen to his words but don't follow some of his examples.

Excellence. A leader needs to foster a culture of excellence throughout the company: a sense that 'just good enough' isn't enough (but conversely not always reaching for perfectionism when that's impossible, and not making the enemy of the good). Chess players have a saying: 'When you see a good move, look for a better one.' That doesn't mean that they spend absurd amounts of time seeking something which may not be there, purely that they keep their minds and eyes open to the possibility of improvement while being aware that if there is none to be found then the fall-back position is still a good one. Keeping an open mind is a good thing, but not so open that your brain falls out (that's part of Temperance too).

Leadership is often about streamlining wherever possible. Working smarter, not harder. I like brief agendas for meetings ideally, because they help keep meetings from disintegrating into the chaos of differing sub-meetings, interesting anecdotes (I'm guilty of doing this too much!) and in many cases the shorter the meeting the better. I was once on a committee which met to research a specific dataset and pass that data back to the main committee. Luckily I found that the exact data had been gathered by others and was up-to-date and exactly what was needed. In the first ten minutes of the meeting I was chairing I said, 'Great, let's pass it on to the bigger committee which will analyse this and incorporate it into their wider findings,' and moved to end the meeting. People were stunned that I'd done so. Some even accused me of being flippant and not taking it seriously. I said, 'We were tasked with doing something, we've done it. That's it.' But the meeting had been scheduled to last a whole morning and probably into lunchtime too, and many of the committee clearly wanted it to do so. Personally I wanted to get out of the room and go and do something, anything, more interesting and productive. Too many people love procrastinating in meetings, or just hearing their own voices, and those kinds of people are exactly the kind of people you shouldn't have in meetings. Do not permit someone to say things along the lines of, 'I'd just like to say that I fully agree with what the last person has just said, and furthermore, for the avoidance of doubt, I'd like to reiterate that I endorse' and et cetera. Words that are sounds with no data value just waste everybody's time. Sadly some people seem to like having their time wasted. Maybe they don't have anything else to do?

If something needs reading beforehand – a report, a memo, whatever – it can be a good idea to start the meeting with everyone actually reading that item, because you can bet that at least half of them won't have done their homework, no matter what they say, and will just try and bluff their way through it like essay crisis students in a tutorial. Elon Musk's advice about meetings is pretty good. 'Get rid of all large meetings, unless you're certain they're providing value to the whole audience, in which case keep them very short. Also get rid of frequent meetings, unless you are dealing with an extremely urgent matter. Meeting frequency should drop rapidly once the urgent matter is resolved. Walk out of a meeting or drop off a call as soon as it is obvious you aren't adding value. It is not rude to leave: it is rude to make someone stay and waste their time.'

Jeff Bezos has a 'two-pizza' rule for meetings: that two pizzas should be enough to feed everyone in the meeting, and if they're not then there are too many people present. This of course depends on the size of the pizza, whether it's a deep crust one, or thin and traditional, and the appetites/metabolisms of those involved, but even a large pizza can feed perhaps half a dozen people at most, so let's say a dozen people maximum. The precise figures, of course, aren't important: it's the principle, which aims to ensure that everyone in a meeting needs to be there, that the meeting won't disintegrate into side meetings, and that everyone whose voice needs to be heard has that chance. The larger the team, the more opinions are proffered and the more difficult it becomes to reach conclusions and make decisions. But conversely you need enough people to challenge an automatic consensus and present alternative viewpoints and ideas. The two-pizza rule is a good balance between the two.

I want people to use common sense – not least because once upon a time common sense was also known as 'horse sense', and horses have better sense than most humans. People make complications where there don't need to be any, and the leader's job is to cut through all that. I have a much valued colleague who came to us from a big corporate company. He understandably wanted to make an impression in the first big meeting; so did I. He worked hard on what he'd been used to doing previously. A full-on, high-octane, turbo-charged 30-page Powerpoint magnum opus. He spent all weekend on it. It was accurate, detailed and professional. I cut him off two minutes in. 'I don't need to hear all this,' I said. 'Just give me the last two pages – your conclusion.' I knew that his methodology and findings would have been sound – I wouldn't have employed him otherwise – so I didn't need to see his process, just the outcome of it. If I wildly disagreed we might well have needed to delve into the other pages to see why, but he is an expert, so treat him like an expert. The look on his face was brilliant; part shock, part realisation that this job was going to be quite a lot different than his last one with many more freedoms and a lot less business waffle. He talks about it even now. Even when Powerpoint presentations are necessary, and they can be helpful, I like to see them used only as guidelines or agenda: there are few things which annoy me more than people reading out words I've read myself two minutes before when they first appeared on screen. I can read much faster than people can talk and I will have read your slide almost instantly when it appeared.

Excellence also comes through good communication channels. Again, Musk is good here. 'Communication should travel via the shortest path necessary to get the job done, not through the chain of command.' Any manager who attempts to enforce chain of command communication will soon find themselves working elsewhere. A major source of issues is poor communication between departments and people who feel empowered to build silos or fiefdoms around their hold on power. The way to solve this is to try to allow free flow of information between levels. It's often as simple as copying others into that email. I find just knowing that someone's talking via email helps me get a feel for data flow. Any decision of significance at Rebellion needs to be made by my brother and I together so when someone forgets to cc Chris or me, and necessitates us having to forward that email to the other, it's annoying and wastes our time, and also if you have to check the list of who the email has been sent to, it wastes even more time.

'If, in order to get something done between departments, an individual contributor has to talk to their manager, who talks to a director, who talks to a VP, who talks to another VP, who talks to a director, who talks to a manager, who talks to someone doing the actual work, then super dumb things will happen. It must be ok for people to talk directly and just make the right thing happen.' Maintaining a chain of command is important, but that chain is there to facilitate things getting done, not get in the way. Communication should be goal oriented.

Self. Former Navy SEAL Jocko Willink said that 'what makes leadership so hard is dealing with people, and people are crazy.

And the craziest person a leader has to deal with is themselves.' It's not a very flattering assessment, perhaps, but it's also probably more accurate than most leaders would like to think.

Being a leader often involves looking outside yourself and considering the needs of other people – your employees, your customers, your suppliers, the media, investors if you have them. It can be easy when you're responsible for and to lots of people to concentrate on them so much that you forget about your own performance. But this is counterproductive. A leader can't demand that his employees keep their own personal performances high and then not do the same themselves. They are just as much part of the company as anyone is, and they need to justify their position as much as anyone else does, if not more. One of the paradoxes of leadership is this: sometimes the best way to lead is to be selfish. Sometimes you need to be thinking of your own needs because it's so easy to be pulled in several different directions at once, losing focus on what is important. You have to learn to say 'no' on occasion, or 'please wait a few days, I'm busy' (which I have often found easier said than done). No organisation worth its salt can afford to carry too many passengers for too long (unless they're a transport company), but sometimes you need to prioritise and clear the decks for a while, without getting bogged down in small details.

There are moments when I concentrate on my own work because I have to, even if this is temporarily at the expense of wider corporate concerns. I could spend every day looking outwards, checking on my staff and so on, but I also have my own job to do, my own creative needs and projects. I like to have an open-door policy in the office – when my door is open anyone is welcome to come in – but sometimes I shut it, and when it's shut I don't want to be disturbed. I shut it for private meetings, obviously, but quite a lot of the time I shut it as I need to work on my own and therefore require concentration. Being disturbed one moment then another jumps you out of the valuable creative zone and focus that is such an important thing to be able to achieve. Book yourself some time without disturbances, literally book them in your calendar before someone finds that useful 'blank' space in your day and puts a meeting there.

I make sure to hold myself to the same standards I hold everyone else to. If I'm honest with, about and to myself, that allows me to instil a culture of honesty all the way through the company, and honesty is absolutely key to good overall performance. I own my mistakes and don't make excuses for them; this encourages others to follow suit, and when everyone in a team is doing that then the environment is healthy and the team has the best chance of improving and performing well.

I don't worry about making mistakes, not for myself or anyone else. Everyone makes mistakes. No one's perfect. The only way not to make a mistake is not to try something in the first place, and that's not how I've ever run a business (or indeed behaved in life). Making a mistake isn't wrong or unprofessional. What *is* wrong and unprofessional is trying to sweep that mistake under the carpet, or ignore it, because by pretending it never happened you deny yourself the opportunity to learn from it next time round, and probably make it even harder to fix up afterwards. Blamestorming in a business is commonplace; everybody seems to like to deflect why something has gone wrong. Whilst that's important to try to discover and not repeat, what's immediately important is to work out how to fix the problem. Ideally I'd like everybody to solution-storm (I need to find a better title for it) and propose ways to deal with whatever it is.

Objective. Objective is both noun and adjective: a goal and impartiality respectively.

As a noun, objectives – goals – are crucial for a leader. You can't lead if you don't know where you're going, how you're getting there, and how you'll know when you've got there. There's no point me saying, 'Oh, we're just going to make this and that cool game, publish these books, and hope they do well.' I need to know what kind of sales we expect, what kind of market we're looking at, what's the timetable for various development stages, what projected turnover and profit figures are, and so on. Only if I know these, and know that they've been calculated reasonably, can I know whether we're performing as we should be, or whether we've completely missed the boat (which happens; very little goes exactly according to plan). Objectives need to be both measurable and achievable, in the short term as well as the medium and long term too. Running a company and looking back is a little bit like going for a long walk, or deciding you want to walk the Pennine Trail, or from Lands End to John O'Groats. If you actually went 'oh it's a long way' you wouldn't bother doing it, but if you walk as far as you can walk sensibly in a day and then go to a B&B or something and then do the next bit, in a few weeks, you'll have walked the distance. Running a business is a bit like that. It's fun to have a milestone – 10th, 20th, 25th, 30th – but what's next? I'm always looking ahead. The past is the past, and we've got to be here now to have a future. Just keep going as best you can and you'll travel far either metaphorically or literally.

Objectivity, when used in the sense of trying to assess things as unbiasedly and dispassionately as possible – is also critical. It's easy to become blind to the truth of things you're involved with, either because you're too close to and invested in them and/or because you've fallen into routines which you don't bother to change as they've always worked well enough up to now. But a good leader will take a step back now and then and ask himself, 'Is this all as good as it can be? Is there anything which can be changed to make things go better?' Often you find that there is. Sometimes I think of this as a bird's eye view of the landscape, other times the view a knight would get from the back of a destrier. Seeing over the heads of the infantry on the battlefield and being able to move rapidly to where the need is the most pressing. Stripping out bias is incredibly hard, as sometimes half the struggle is recognising that the bias is there in the first place. We're all guilty to some degree of cognitive biases. Things like the sunk cost fallacy, where good money is spent after bad money, so doubling down on the potential losses. Cognitive biases are errors in the way the human brain works, and recognising that they exist is one way of reducing their impacts.

Luck. I've been lucky enough to be in at more or less the birth of an entire field of the media. A new industry based on new technology as well as the birth of our new company, so I've seen not just who's made it and who hasn't but *why* too. Perspective is sometimes much clearer in the rear-view mirror, though less useful than looking forwards. Success is down to many things – talent, timing, persistence, but the one no-one likes to talk about is luck. This is understandable. As a species we like to think that we can control pretty much everything in our immediate orbit, and the vast majority of narratives we consume – certainly fictional narratives – have moral overtones: good people triumph, bad people get their comeuppance, hard work is rewarded, everyone gets their just desserts, and so on. But real life isn't often like that. It's much more chaotic and random. There's no locked-in correlation between effort, quality and success. They're correlated, obviously, but also sometimes you can put hard work into something and it still not be of premium quality; sometimes you can make something great but for whatever reason it doesn't fly in the marketplace; sometimes a project has great commercial success even though you may think it's not as good as other things you've done.

Whether something has been a financial success or a failure is certainly not the only thing which defines it. A success can be fluky and in practical terms undeserved; a failure can be unlucky. The Battle of Agincourt in 1415 might have turned out very differently if it hadn't rained so heavily beforehand; just look at what happened at Patay a few decades later, which is, understandably from the English perspective, much less well known or discussed. At Agincourt, or Azincourt as it is still known today, the French had planned to use the narrowness of the battlefield to their advantage, but instead, according to some historians, they found themselves encumbered by their heavy armour and sinking in the deep mud. Just walking forwards to engage the enemy must have been a huge effort. This had several knock-on effects, all following on from each other in turn. Sinking in the mud meant that they were exhausted by the time they reached the English lines (and some did). Exhaustion meant that many fell and even drowned in the mud. The bodies made it harder for those behind to manoeuvre, exposing them to carefully aimed arrows in turn. A longbowman is likely to be able to place an arrow into a small target from about 30 yards away in my opinion. Aiming at the gaps in plate coverage, the wrists, knee joints from the side, armpits, the palms of hands and temporary gaps caused by struggling movement or stumbles. It was a litany of woes which all began with heavy rainfall. On a dry day, who knows what would have happened? I've jousted at Azincourt field during one of the re-enactments there and the mud in the adjoining field was, as far as I can remember, reddish clay and very sticky.

It's tempting to think that the result is all that matters and in some way preordained. But that's not true. The good leader looks beyond the result and assesses the processes and events which led up to that result. What went well? What could have been done better? How were we lucky? What did we forget? What can we learn for next time?

Usefulness. As one of the big bosses (as my brother and I are frequently called) you can, perhaps weirdly, feel less valued than those you're in charge of, as you're guiding and nudging the work of many others, often through the work of sub-managers or even sub-sub-managers. Things get lost in translation too. It's tempting for managers to get down and dirty on the business front line: after all, it's that kind of job which probably got them to where they are now. But if that manager thinks back to when they did indeed have that job, they'll also remember how much they'd disliked having a manager always getting involved in the tiny detail. A manager's job is to co-ordinate the talented people they're in charge of and challenge and support them so that they can do their jobs, and to do them as well as possible. That doesn't involve hovering every second of every day, micromanaging every last detail, and interfering to the extent of doing their workers' jobs for them: if the latter's the case then clearly one of you need not be employed. Having said that, there is a balance to be achieved in keeping an eye on the detail to the right level, but giving the team freedom to achieve the things they need to achieve. The amount of involvement will vary from personality to personality and you need to stay alert to varying the input as needed. Often junior staff will need more input at the beginning than senior ones, though the decisions senior staff will need to make may have bigger impacts on the team goal.

I'm hands on, and I try to play all the games we release as they're made, and as they're developed. My input to a project is only one of many other people's: it's not automatically right, better or more valuable just because I'm the boss. I'm wary of what some people disparagingly label 'seagull management'; when you swoop in, shit on everyone, knock things over and fly off again. I'd like to swoop in, provide exquisitely accurate targeted insight and then glide away again gracefully. Maybe we can call that hawk management? Maybe there's another more suitable type of bird that could be used. And now I'm thinking about what a hummingbird management style might be, or indeed a totally financially driven vulture management, let alone penguin management? I hope that at the very least I'm appreciated by my employees, irrespective of the exact ornithological designation they give me. I certainly try to look at things with a commercial eye: not nakedly and exclusively so, but hopefully without pretension or snobbery too. Since we have many very successful games under our belts, and many number one hits, I think I can confidently say our ideas are validated by the marketplace and the game-playing public.

Teamwork. A good business leader acts as an enabler and a force multiplier for everyone else, ensuring that they are not just improving their own individual performances but that of the collective too: that everyone is more efficient, that they see opportunities earlier and get to them quicker than the competition does.

Teamwork is of course a *sine qua non* of any successful team – as the old cliché goes, there's no 'I' in 'team' (unless you write in squared-off block capitals and colour in the inside of the A) – and many of my thoughts about it are covered in the next point, *Inclusivity*. So here's a slightly different angle. One of the hardest things to deal with in terms of teamwork is the Peter Principle, where people are promoted to one level above their natural competence: that is, they do a succession of jobs well enough to earn promotion to the next one, but eventually they find a level beyond their capabilities and that's where they stay, as they won't get promoted (not good enough) nor demoted (corporate inertia and employment law).

As a senior manager who's focussing on the big picture, trusting the people beneath you to do their jobs, you can miss these kinds of things, and therefore miss the opportunity to deal with them, until they've been going on a long time. It's not that these people are woefully incompetent – those ones are easy to spot and easy to deal with. It's the ones who are just either side of OK, who don't do too much wrong but don't do too much standout right either, who are the hardest ones to deal with. Do you keep them in place because they're doing no harm and because replacement equals disruption, especially if there's no ready-made or obvious replacement? Do you get people to work around them and cover for their inadequacies? It would of course be nice to think that you would never settle for anything other than the best, but that also depends on your options and alternatives. Armies need people to dig latrines and empty the rubbish after all. Not every soldier is in the SAS.

Inclusivity. 'Leadership,' said Dwight D. Eisenhower, 'is the art of getting someone else to do something you want done because he wants to do it.' That's a bit too cynical for me, and smacks of deception. Being a leader shouldn't be about laying down the law and expecting people to obey without question. *Oderint dum metuant*, Caligula is reputed to have said: let them hate, so long as they fear. A viable life strategy for a Roman emperor, perhaps, but less likely to gain traction in today's corporate world. If people only do what you tell them to because they're scared of you, then they'll only do what you tell them for as long as they're scared of you. One day either that fear will go, or they will realise that things are now so bad that they haven't got much left to lose. Either way, the leader loses everything when that moment comes.

In contrast, a leader who makes the army happy empowers them to keep going on their own accord. Treat them with respect and listen to feedback, and not only will you keep them happy, but you'll also improve the performance of your team, which is – or should be – your ultimate aim. Leadership is, in part, about persuasion. Persuasion involves hearts as well as minds, and that can't all be done by one person with no help from anyone else. All successful leadership is shared leadership. That doesn't mean that the ultimate authority of the top person is threatened or undermined: it means that they have got other senior or influential people in the organisation to buy into their vision. Any successful company will have leaders at every level.

Rather than feel threatened by that, I use it to my advantage. I've never been interested in being right for my own sake: I want us to collectively come up with the best ways forward. I might well have to choose between two fairly reasonable alternatives and disappoint someone in the process. A leader who feels threatened by those beneath them will hoard responsibility and power: a leader genuinely concerned for the team will delegate and give people roles but hold them accountable too. Any leader who wants to take everything on themselves and not trust anybody else to do anything is harming the team and making it all about themselves, in which case they shouldn't be leader in the first place. Because no leader can do it all themselves. It doesn't matter how experienced, intelligent, prepared or committed you are. There's no point any one person trying to control everything to the finest detail: that just puts huge stress on them. Every leader needs input from other people to allow them to make the best decisions possible. They need perspective, and they can only get that perspective by consulting others. These others won't just give the leader good advice; they'll give fresh and interesting viewpoints too, because their personalities, their experiences and their areas of expertise will be different not just from the leader's but from each other's too. There'll always be people who know things you don't and have ways of doing things well that you don't. This is why I try to empower people with micro-projects – not for the sake of them but because they need doing, and furnishing someone with ownership of a challenge is a very good way of ensuring they're proud of their work and motivated to do it as well as they can. Dividing a big project up into smaller, more achievable sub-goals is a good technique.

An army usually has at least two sets of hierarchies: one within the ranks of the non-commissioned soldiers and one for the officers. That may well be optimal for an armed forces organisation, but in business such rigid vertical hierarchy is almost always counter-productive. A business – at least a small or medium-sized one – is better off thinking of itself more along the lines of the SAS structure. When a soldier goes from the regular army to the SAS – or, as they call it, from the Green Army to the Regiment – ranking becomes far less important. All non-commissioned soldiers start again at the rank of Private, all officers take a demotion of a rank, and the interplay between them all becomes much more informal, with the recognition that good ideas can come from anywhere and everywhere and the acceptance that everyone involved is very good at what they do. It's not the actual elimination of rank which is important here, but the effect which that elimination has.

In the William Morris agency, there was a tradition that everyone there started in the post room no matter who they were. I don't know if it still exists, or to what extent it was ever universally applied – it's hard to imagine a senior executive parachuted in from outside and told to spend a month or so in the post room – but the principles behind it are good ones: that everyone is treated equally, and that every part of the company does an important and worthwhile job.

Overview. It's easy to get bogged down in detail, but it's your duty to make sure everyone's marching in the right direction, and ideally in step (unless it's over a bridge): it's your moral obligation as leader to have an elevated broad view and a plan of battle. You should drive the overall strategy but in an ideal world leave the tactics to sub-leaders. You're not the one getting covered in mud and shit like your foot soldiers, though at certain times of history, leaders were very much expected to be front and centre of the battle line. As a general, you shouldn't really need to be focussed on tiny details as they necessarily draw your gaze away from the overview too much. (I'm sometimes bemused by the title CEO, Chief Executive Officer, because for me that label can carry negative baggage with it. Sometimes we've joked about changing our titles for more interesting, if less understandable, titles. How about Benevolent Despot For Life, Grand Panjandrum, High Ninja Master, or Most Beloved Leader? Something like that: more Ruritanian than North Korean, obviously. But I digress.)

Conversely and possibly ironically, considering what I've

just said about broad views, sometimes the higher you get in an organisation, the narrower your data set can be in some ways. Often you only get to hear what others want you to hear and on occasion I've wished I had more regular and casual communications with a wider range of colleagues. It's important to maintain contacts as much as possible with other people in your organisation and foster an atmosphere of communication and mutual respect (easier said than done as usual). As companies grow they can become siloed. Power structures develop, sometimes unintentionally, sometimes because a manager's personality means they want to control the flow of information, and it's easy to forget that not everybody has the same data as you do. But the latter is critical. An elevated position is only as good as the use you make of it. For knights in armour on the medieval battlefield, sitting on a horse meant they could see over the heads of the foot soldiers, way more strategically than they could have otherwise, and could move themselves and their forces more quickly to where they were needed. Cavalry has two main advantages over infantry: height, so you can see further, and speed, so you can be somewhere faster than walking. It's not so much that they could see further in absolute terms – the difference in the visible horizon for a man on foot as opposed to on horseback is about a mile – but that they could see over the usual head-height obstructions (other people, usually).

That vision can provide huge advantages. Wayne Gretzky, probably the greatest ice-hockey player in history, was once asked the secret of his success. He explained that he wasn't the quickest player, or the strongest, or the best skater. What really made him good was the advice his dad had given him as a young boy: 'Don't skate to where the puck is. Skate to where the puck will be.' It was Gretzky's anticipation which set him apart from everyone else, and the higher your view the better your chances of anticipating and shaping changes and future success.

There are other ways of viewing this, too. For example, a well-known internet meme shows a wolf pack moving through a snowy landscape. The caption goes something like this. 'A wolf pack. The first three are the old or sick: they give the pace to the entire pack. If it was the other way round, they would be left behind, losing contact with the pack. In case of an ambush they would be sacrificed. Then come five strong ones, the front line. In the centre are the rest of the pack members, then the five strongest following. Last is alone, the alpha. He controls everything from the rear. In that position he can see everything, decide the direction. He sees all of the pack. The pack moves according to the elders' pace and help each other, watch each other.'

The caption's inaccurate – that's not how wolves work, and if they do have an alpha animal it's down to that animal's status as the main breeder rather than any inherent leadership qualities – but the very fact that it's been written at all demonstrates the appeal of the 'leading from the back' concept. It can also be seen in the famous book *Watership Down*, about a tribe of rabbits who flee their warren. Their chief rabbit Hazel is not the biggest, strongest, cleverest or the best fighter, but by letting those rabbits who are each of those use their abilities as best they can, he proves himself the ideal leader. And that, in the end, is what it's all about. A leader is judged not by their own actions usually, but by more often those of the people around them. By the way the book *Watership Down* is marvellous. Don't be put off reading it because of the frightening animation that was made from it. I was for too long, and re-read the masterpiece only fairly recently. The stories are quite different in many details and there's nothing terrifying about the book; it's very uplifting and inspirational.

Nucleus. There's an old saying that 'the fish rots from the head' – that is, if a leader is weak, corrupt or venal then eventually those values will be passed down the line and corrode the organisation in question. (I'm not sure that a fish does in fact rot from the head. My guess would be that it rots from its internal organs first, but it's a colourful expression and fish does smell pretty alarming when rotten.) But of course the opposite is also true: good things come down from the top too. As a leader, you are not just the apex of the pyramid but the nucleus around which others orbit too (if that's not too confusing an image): all departments sooner or later report to you. The junk bond king Michael Milken was famous in the '80s for having a vast X-shaped array of desks in his firm, with him sitting at the centre where all four quarters met. That was almost certainly just for show and PR purposes, I bet, and selling junk bonds was all about positioning and confidence. I don't go that far in the slightest, but I do know that what I do ripples outwards as well as downwards, so I try to make sure those effects are positive ones.

A leader ought to be upbeat. Teams take their emotional cues from the leaders, and both positivity and negativity radiate downwards and outwards very fast. I'm lucky in that my default nature is upbeat – I'm a glass-half-full person and always try look on the optimistic side of any situation, even if it's a bad thing that's just happened. In a bad happenstance, I try to work out how to make the best of that situation or turn it around to our advantage, or gain some kind of upside, even if it's very minor. You can't and won't always win, but you can try valiantly to treat defeat as a springboard. On balance I think it has become easy to me to be positive, and sometimes that can be to my detriment when judging the actions of others. I like to believe most people are decent and well meaning, but some just aren't. There's no point being positive unless you show it and communicate it outwards. What you're thinking may not be obvious to others. Praising people when they've done well is important. It seems to be one of those things that's so obvious they go without saying, but a lot of things which go without saying end up being unsaid. Leadership for me is far more about carrot than stick. The majority of people respond better to praise than criticism: they like to know that their efforts are both recognised and appreciated. The majority of horses too respond to positive reinforcement and kind treatment better in the long run. Fear training with a horse can work, but there will always be something a horse will fear more than you. Positive training, encouragement, will give the horse confidence in you and itself to deal with the fear well. It turns out that people are not that different to horses, though arguably they're slower to learn.

Of course, praise should be both genuine and selective. A leader who praises their workers for every small thing they do – that is, effectively, for showing up and doing their jobs – will find that the currency of that praise becomes devalued very quickly indeed. Nor should you praise just for the sake of morale. Praise and achievement should ideally be an endless feedback loop: good people doing their jobs well and therefore earning praise which keeps them feeling valued and motivated to continue achieving. Sometimes just saying a simple thank you to someone can be valued more than you think. We all like doing something well and being appreciated for it.

Criticism is a trickier one, if only because praise and criticism slightly remind me of the first line of *Anna Karenina* about happy and unhappy families. The majority of people accept praise the same way (with slight variations due to embarrassment, self-criticism etc), but everyone deals with criticism differently. A good leader recognises this, responds to it and tailors their responses accordingly. Some people take things very personally and need an arm round the shoulder, others ask for detailed feedback so they can see exactly where they went wrong, and others still need a solid metaphorical kick up the arse from time to time. As a side note don't kick an equine; they're very much better than you at kicking, as I know well from a certain mule I have in training who goes by the name 'the Mule with no name'. He kicks exactly as you'd expect. I had difficulty walking for a few days. My left gluteus maximus changed colour.

The one thing I've never held with is bawling people out in public. It's always struck me as something that's counterproductive in every way: it shames the person on the receiving end and therefore makes them less likely to work well (if only through fear of making more mistakes), it embarrasses and discomforts the rest of the workforce, and it cements any image of the manager as an egotistic bully. If you have to criticise someone, take them into your office and do so behind closed doors. If your criticism is of the workforce in general, then you should be looking at yourself as much as you are them, since collective failure is by definition also a failure of leadership.

The language I use with co-workers is important too. I can't abide management-speak: it obfuscates, complicates and patronises. I always try to speak to my employees the way I'd speak to anyone, and to connect with them on a normal level. There are certain acronyms which are widely used and well understood in the games industry, so I use them in context, but in general I try to steer away from them or other nonsense words. I particularly hate verbing of nouns too. Anything that requires an explanation inhibits communication. I have been known to interrupt presentations and loudly ask what a certain acronym means, partly because I don't actually know, and partly because it annoys me that they haven't considered that their audience may not know. At least use the full phrase before dropping the ruddy acronym, and if the acronym takes as long to say at the actual thing then don't use it.

Finally, not everyone's a leader, and not everyone wants to be. It's not a criticism of someone to say that they're a follower rather than a leader: by definition most people are followers. In the right circumstances I'm a follower too. If you don't have the personality or inclination for it, then there's not only no point trying to force you into a position of leadership: it'll actually be counterproductive. The flipside of this is that sometimes you don't know you're a natural leader until it's put to the test: it's often other people who see it in you before you do yourself. Either way, just be yourself. If you're not, sooner or later you'll get found out, and people don't respect frauds. I do seem to instinctively take a leading role, even when I really don't want to do that. There's something in me that just has difficulty not getting involved.

Chapter Eight

Truth

THE MEDIEVAL KNIGHT was enjoined by the rules of chivalry, at all times to speak the truth, not just by way of integrity but because it was felt there was no honour in lying to protect others. Of course lying is not the same as not saying anything at all. I'm not sure whether speaking the truth bluntly at all times without care for what people think or feel is an entirely plausible way to live. Sometimes things have to be said without dressing them up or softening them, but at other times it's perfectly acceptable to say that this is something you don't want to discuss or which makes you feel uncomfortable. Both of those are a long way from lying. Deliberate lies erode your claims to be seen as a trustworthy individual or an honest broker, and that goes even when the lies appear small or inconsequential. As mentioned earlier, I don't play golf, but I understand from those who do that you can tell a lot about someone's character by their willingness to lie about their score or to move their ball to make the shot a bit easier. Fudging on the little rules weakens the fabric of society for everyone. It's also hard to remember lies, especially if you've told them without thinking. When I was a student, I remember being witness to a police officer interviewing a shoplifting suspect outside a shop. They asked them their name, wrote it down, asked several more questions, then asked them their name again. The suspect couldn't immediately remember their earlier lie. That's a clever, and simple, technique I thought. Then my bus turned up and I got on and never found out the outcome, but I suspect they were arrested so they could at least be identified. 'Oh what a tangled web we weave when first we practise to deceive', as Sir Walter Scott (not Shakespeare) actually wrote.

Truth is particularly important when it comes to how you treat your colleagues. I covered part of this in the previous chapter about leadership, but whereas leadership is as much internal as external, this is more about the externalities of interpersonal relationships. The actual way in which you relate to people is important. It's important too that it's a kind and honest communication in my opinion. Chris and I have slightly different temperaments. He's more technical and methodical, and I'm more emotional and extraverted (sometimes, so I think). One is not better than the other, obviously. Those contrasting temperaments complement each other and working with Chris is brilliant, but we do occasionally have differences. If we can't resolve them, we are mostly grown up about things. Mostly. When we were a lot younger, we did, on occasion, settle things by wrestling.

I want to have fun and learn, as I think learning should be a lifelong thing to do. Working with skilful, enthusiastic and good people is an absolute pleasure. Working with difficult, morose or bad people is hard, and the hassle involved is disproportionately large. I believe it's generally a benefit to have a reputation for being decent and positive, as in situations of narrow or no margins, that may well tip a decision in your favour. If you're objectionable then you have to be a genius or very lucky to get away with it, but few people are (geniuses, that is. Lots of people are objectionable). If you have happy people making products they want to make, broadly speaking you get a better output from people. I like the ideal of everybody waking up on Monday morning and thinking 'Great!' On Sunday evenings I usually get quite excited about the week ahead and what opportunities and experiences it will bring; not always of course, that would be odd, but more often than not.

I'm very aware that the example Chris and I set filters down throughout the company. In the mid-1990s our one major customer went bust, having not paid us. They owed us pretty much all the money we were going to earn that year, well in excess of £100,000. My brother and I paid the ten staff we had at the time with our personal savings. It was a very painful experience. We managed to secure another client within five months, after rushing around the country and the US and Japan, telling people we had the resources available and trying not to sound desperate. We actually found a better partner to work with, but we had six months of stress when we really did not know what would happen. The really important bit, however, was that we looked after our staff and showed them we would go the extra mile for them.

I still remember the first member of staff we employed: Justin Rae, who later became very big in the video game giant Electronic Arts and now runs his own design studio. It was a strange kind of obligation, hiring someone and being responsible for their livelihood: so strange, in fact, that I almost wasn't sure how to speak to him. (The answer was, of course, to speak to him perfectly normally.) As the industry gets older, you find yourself in the situation where some of our staff have been with us for more than two decades. Some have a family and kids at school or university. As a business owner, you have to be really careful. Sometimes, in extremis, you have to lay people off, or close an area of business, but you shouldn't do it lightly or easily. It's a genuinely horrible situation to be in as a leader. You have to think about the ramifications and personal impacts of your strategic decisions. We're not just mucking around with young people's lives where if they get fired, they can just push off to Montreal, Paris, Hong Kong and start again. Potentially, if things go wrong, we're affecting our staff, their partners and their children. It's a sobering thought if you care about people. Sometimes you do think, 'Oh, can we just be small again?'

Being the appropriate size is an important aspect of any company. I like the idea of having a big-ish company: you can achieve ambitious things. But I like the idea of everyone making a difference too. I don't want to have a thousand people and not know any of them. I don't want to have a faceless workforce where I can't talk to them and they can't talk to me. We want to do more games, but we don't want to do too many games. So far our expansion is working well for us. Our games cost a decent chunk of money to make, many tens of millions, but make an even more decent chunk of money in return. We make a profit and we plough that profit back into staff, training people, making new games, and that for me is it. That's what we want to do.

No company starts out as a big company, even if they grow very quickly. Tensions often happen when one company acquires another and cultures clash. I've always been very aware of this when we've bought other companies and integrated them and their staff into the Rebellion family. Some companies have a tight culture: rigid hierarchy, centralised decision-making, concentration on hours worked, strict rules and processes, insisting on a way of dressing, or which door to use to get into the office. Others are much looser, and we're one of the latter types. Companies reflect the values of those who founded them and those who run them. I'm laissez-faire and not a great believer in authoritarian structures: I accept that you need a hierarchy, but like to remain as flexible within that as possible, and I encourage communication across the company. It's easy to copy someone into an email; it takes much more time to realise someone should be in that communication loop and forward an email to them. I once mistakenly left my phone unsilenced when in a museum. The thing rang. I swiftly silenced it and spoke briefly to the caller that I'd ring them back and headed for the exit. An obstreperous, and probably bored, member of staff loudly told me that I 'could not use the phone in the museum'. I was just leaving quietly having disturbed almost no-one. The staff member was causing a scene. I replied, 'I most certainly can use a phone in here, but I believe the term you wanted to use is "I ought not to use it" and now you've caused much more fuss by your behaviour than my original brief transgression did. Well done.'

Neither model is in itself right or wrong, but left unchecked both can have disadvantages: tight cultures find it hard to adapt and change, loose cultures can be disorganised, and either of these can lead to missed opportunities and sub-optimal performance. When Chris and I look at a company with a view to buying it, we don't just look at the balance sheet and the financials: we look at the culture too. How do they work? What do the staff expect? Where are the differences between their culture and ours? How much would they have to sacrifice of that – and, conversely, how much would we have to, and how much can we learn from them? Tightness can be made more flexible, looseness can be made more structured. When Pixar was bought by Disney in 2006, part of the deal was that Pixar could keep aspects of their looser culture: they didn't have to sign individual employment contracts with Disney, they could choose their own job titles, they could decorate their offices how they liked, and they continued their annual paper aeroplane contest. Small things, perhaps, but people notice and value the small things.

Of course this cultural integration is not simply a one-time agreement between both sides at the time of the merger or buyout: it has to be monitored and tweaked as time goes by. Sometimes it simply doesn't work. We took over the studio which made *Lara Croft*, and some people there had the attitude that 'we made *Lara Croft*, therefore everything we do is perfect'. I then found out that some of those people with that attitude hadn't even worked on the games themselves in the first place. Claiming the valour of other people is a big no-no for me, and in the end, after a lot of hard work and attempts at problem solving, we had to make the difficult decision to shut the studio down. It was a good, if very unpleasant and expensive, lesson: I tried so hard to shift the attitude of those teams, but there were too many entrenched belief systems there and I just couldn't do it.

In medieval times knights were rewarded with land and money to fight for the king. However, not all of them were especially good at fighting or especially keen to do so, and so a system called scutage came in (from the Latin word 'scutum', meaning 'shield'), by which knights essentially bought themselves out of the obligation to fight and paid to hire mercenaries instead, which, if you're not a good fighter, was probably better for the king's army anyway. It was the first separation of knighthood from direct combat obligations, and helped gradually secure the separation of aristocracy from nobility. Both owned land, but the aristocrats increasingly had the wealth while the nobles still went to war. Whoever they were, though, knights needed staff and people, just as businesses do today. Sometimes commentators suggest that the medieval period is represented by three types of people. Those who fought, those who prayed and those who worked. (It wasn't that neat and simple in fact, but it's a useful generalisation.) Shares, share dealing and the stockmarket all started in the late medieval period after all. Workers worked fewer hours than we do today overall and were taxed less too. Most tax was based on land holding, so if you didn't have any land, you didn't pay most tax, though you did have feudal obligations. They also had more free time, holy days and festivals. They had a lot of festivals, and it seems pretty much every day was a holy day of one obscure saint or another. Agricultural workers, the peasantry, who made up about ninety percent or more of the population, were held as very important but slightly 'other' by the ruling class, who in a patrician kind of way liked to make decisions for little people. Workers were valued in the same way as a really good horse and sword were valued. In that kind of agrarian society there was much more closeness to death and life: when you have to kill your own food, perhaps killing other humans isn't that big a step.

One thing's for sure: knights would never have used the modern term 'human resources', let alone the even more egregious abominations such as 'human capital management'. Staff aren't simply resources or capital to be managed. They're people, and I sincerely hope I never treat them as anything else, though we do have an HR department of course. I hate all kinds of other bad HR-speak, such as 'aligning HR goals with business goals'. The two for me are exactly the same, as without the people who work for me I literally have no business; 'organisational change manager' (that's my job as CEO, and I don't need someone else to do it for me), 'competencies' (competence is the very least anyone should expect of an employee), 'engagement' (see 'competencies'), 'downsizing/rightsizing/streamlining/optimising/outsourcing' (if you're going to sack someone at least have the bottle to call it what it is: no euphemism fools someone who's just lost their job) and that catch-all so mercilessly and rightly lampooned by *Private Eye*, 'solutions' (to describe what happens when you do your job properly). HR, when done well, is very valuable; when done badly it has a very negative impact on an organisation.

I've never had a PA or secretary. I've never wanted one; I'm more efficient without one, and I suspect that some people who have them do so at least partly because they enjoy the power and perceived importance which come with having them. I couldn't care less. I'm perfectly capable of making my own appointments, sending my own e-mails and making my own phone calls. The last point especially is something which really annoys me – when you receive a call (it's usually from someone 'important' in the USA, often from that area of business encapsulated as 'Hollywood') and it's someone's assistant saying 'please hold for X'. Then a few moments later X comes on. So X values me so much that not only can they not be bothered to dial my number (which these days is a simple one-click job), but they take up some of my time in waiting for them to deign to come on the line? That's either simply inconsiderate or a deliberate basic positioning power play. Either way, I want no part of it.

Also, a PA ends up being a chamberlain or gatekeeper, and sooner or later they end up being more powerful than the principal rather than vice versa (quite often without the principal knowing at all). Being the one who restricts access, be that access of people or information, is an incredibly powerful position. They're really in charge of you rather than vice versa. They often think they're being protective and doing their job, which they may well be, but it's their priorities rather than yours which come to the fore. For example, a gatekeeper may well be faced with a staff member's mental health problem and decide that this is something for HR rather than me: but I'd want to know that for myself, I'd want to see how I could help, because that staff member works for me and I feel responsible for their well-being.

So much of work is performative if you let it be. On one occasion in LA I had a meeting with Bill Block, at the time an agent for ICM (International Creative Management). A *Vanity Fair* article about him had said, 'He lives his life being an agent. No wife, no kids, no pets of his own: just clients and more clients and deals and more deals. He thinks like a shark. Without forward motion, he will die.'

That alone should have warned me what the place would be like. It was like *Miami Vice*, with everyone – interns included – wearing Armani suits and designer T-shirts. (The interns, I discovered, were paying to be there rather than vice versa.)

'I've arranged a five-minute meeting with Bill,' an assistant said.

'Fuck off,' I replied.

'Excuse me?'

'I said, "fuck off". Five minutes isn't a meeting. It's an introduction.'

'Oh, that's not his shortest meeting slot.'

'It isn't?'

'Oh no. He has two-and-a-half minute power meetings.'

I ended up getting half an hour, simply from refusing to go along with this bullshit, but even so it was still an amusing farce, in terms of it being a performance, a mummery, a show staged for my benefit rather than it being useless. Bill had two assistants pacing up and down with headsets behind him the whole time taking calls. He ate from a bowl of raw garlic cloves (I thought they were macadamia nuts to start with). Maybe he thought I was a vampire. At one stage he took a call when he was mid-sentence with me, spoke to the person on the other end, and then resumed our conversation at the exact point it had paused. It was a call from Steven (I was told later Mr. Spielberg, as the use of 'power first names' was part of the play, and I think it possible it wasn't a real call). But it was all platitudes, all smoke and mirrors: a performance to prove how important he was to his assistants if not to me: a pretence of exclusivity and busyness (as opposed to business) which all amounted to the same thing, a kidology that I needed them more than they needed me. I walked out of the building knowing that the meeting had been illuminating, fascinating, educational and also pointless. We'd likely never do any business together, Hollywood style agents and the computer games industry don't gel well, and that the best I could hope for was that one day I'd be able to tell the story in a book like this.

It was all part of a piece with other aspects I disliked. In Hollywood it's how deals are seen by outside people that matters more than you might guess. High staff turnover and ambitious executives means that the person who made the deal quite likely won't still be there when the substance of that deal has to be delivered. On a similar note, I hate inflation of job titles too, designed to make everyone look more important, because in the end they make people look ridiculous in a Gilbert and Sullivan way. A vice-president in a US firm is pretty much a receptionist, or so it seems, and a managing director may as well be the intern. These phrases – 'managing director', 'vice-president' – are, or should be, reasonably exclusive ones denoting seniority and responsibility, but they're thrown around like confetti. And everyone knows this. When I go to America, there's no point me saying that I'm creative director or anything. They only respond to three big titles – CEO, chairman or (co)founder, as founder shares give you rights. Amusingly I'm all three.

There's a lot of talk now post-pandemic (which seems to be where we're heading at the time of writing) of the office as being a thing of the past, people working from home much more often and as a default position. Of course people should be able from work from home when they can't come in or when there's no reason for them to be in the office that day, but for many people some of the time the office environment is a crucial part both of their individual role and the collective effort. There's a great community aspect to being in the same place which with the best will in the world isn't replicable even by constant Zoom meetings. In the office people feel like colleagues, outside it they feel more like freelancers (a fun medieval phrase, where a knight and colleagues are literally free to provide services to whoever they want, and not obligated to one lord in particular). The power of soft information exchange is a strong one: there's a difference between communicating purely to exchange information and communicating in person, where information comes out more naturally and ends up being more valuable for that very reason.

One generic mistake I recommend avoiding is to employ people in a rush, finding out they were good at interview but not necessarily good at doing the job. Sometimes, it's better to have a vacancy for a while if the alternative is that the fit might be wrong. Just to get someone, anyone, to sit in that seat, is a very bad way of thinking. This is particularly true in our case, because computer game making is such a specialised industry. We need people who are both technical and capable of solving and thinking around problems. Computer games are a blend of pretty much every other form of creative media. We use painting techniques. We have animators. We have music composers and audio engineers. We need choreographers, actors and script writers. We need people who can build a 3D world in real time and render it on commercially available computers. We need professional game players in the quality assurance department to represent the consumer and tell us if we've got something wrong. Technology has become so sophisticated that in the past decade each computer game of the scale that we do, which sells worldwide, will take more than 200 people of different skills about three years to make. These skills include programming, art, games design, animation and sound, each with many sub disciplines. So a quick interview and gut instinct is not enough.

WE COULD LEARN from medieval times in the way they approached things. Knights did an apprenticeship, though it wasn't called that (it was called being a squire). They learned to maintain armour, sharpen weapons, handle horses. They also learned how to behave in polite society, how to eat and drink, how to dance and speak to others. There's a wonderful little medieval book all about etiquette for boys. It suggests not grabbing food with the whole fist, not picking the nose at the table, avoiding speaking when the mouth is full, and alarmingly to avoid scratching vigorously whilst seated at the table. This knightly training began around the age of twelve to fourteen, and ended between nineteen and twenty-one, so it wasn't unlike secondary education today. The importance of preparation can also be seen when it comes to medieval armour, to which there were many parts. Greaves went around the calf and shin; cuisse covered the thighs: tassets provided further protection for the upper thigh and acted as an over plate to the flexible junction between leg and torso, as well as protecting the arming points, the tough cordage that attached the steel plates to the underjacket. A plackart protected the lower torso or belly. There was a mail skirt and a breastplate; the vambraces protect the arm, both upper and lower canons of the same, the couter the elbow protection (an amusing word for readers from the USA) allowing movement in the elbow while protecting the gaps too (there was often more protection on the left arm, where the knight expected more threats, than on the right arm which held the lance); the pauldrons cover the shoulders while the bevor looked after the throat and neck. There are many more specialist terms for medieval armour; some are amusing, as they often derive from a bad English mispronunciation of a French word. The rear end is protected by a cullet plate, literally an arse plate in French. There's clear crossover between that and the armour which modern police officers wear for anti-riot situations. Today's equipment is lighter, chunkier and arguably easier to put on, but in essence the human body hasn't changed materially in all this time: we still have four limbs, a torso and a head. Police anti-riot armour is built to protect against different threats too, and though it'd be better than nothing against medieval weapons, it wouldn't be very good. It's also a lot cheaper to make, and probably comes in three sizes, small medium and large. I bet it fits where it touches. Medieval high status armour is expensive and made to measure. We have a letter from a German knight (well, before the creation of Germany, but the same geographically), in which he complains of his armour chafing, having fought in it, swum back across a moat and walked three miles back to base after a failed attempt to scale a castle wall. The other point about some armour is that often it is better to have someone else help you put it on and check it's fitted properly. Originally this would have been done by squires, but with modern police armour it's just a colleague, which reinforces camaraderie and bonding just as the wearing of armour increases morale and makes for better warriors. The way armour both ancient and modern fits together is a good metaphor for how a company should run: covering all bases, protective in depth and layers, but also allowing flexibility.

There are other similarities between the organisational structure used by medieval knights and today's workplace. Since a 'lance' was the collective noun for a group of fighters, centred about the heavily armed knight himself, so 'freelancers' were those who would roam the land looking for gainful employment. At a time when there weren't standing armies, these free companies were a valuable and sometimes troublesome resource. A knight was the head of a lance, assisted by men at arms who had lower quality equipment and less good horses. The analogy has its limits: for instance, post-medieval armies often had a designated whoremaster or general of harlots to keep both actual prostitutes and other women in order, as they were all deemed 'riotous' and 'prone to distract the men'. The terms whore and harlot seemed to be used mostly descriptively rather than pejoratively as they would be today, and the job title involved keeping some sense of order amongst all the women followers of the army. Not just sex workers, but washerwomen, seamstresses, and likely wives and girlfriends.

A lance then, with the key role of knight at its centre, is rather like a motor racing team today, with the knight as the driver but everyone doing other vital jobs, or a professional cycling team which has a leader and *domestiques* (literally, servants) who work hard for that leader and in turn take a share of whatever prize money he wins.

The idea of unnecessary formality I find quite abhorrent. I will turn up to meetings with government ministers in a shirt and jeans. And I've got long hair. If they don't want to take a meeting with somebody because of what I'm wearing, that's cool by me. I will just turn around and go. Their loss as they wanted a meeting because of what I know, not what I'm wearing. So I don't get bothered about what people wear: often the only time I ever see my employees in a suit is when they come to interview. As long as their clothing keeps them warm, protects them and doesn't offend anyone, that's fine. I have asked someone to change once when the T-shirt they were wearing displayed a logo and design that was grossly offensive to a certain group of people. A lot of people at work take their shoes off and walk around in their socks. I couldn't care less. Occasionally we have had Lego-related foot incidents at work. People keep toys on their desks after all.

Up to a certain point both eccentricity and charisma are good for business. They help people remember you and provide anecdotes for others to speak about which helps keep your business in the forefront of their minds, at least a little. Medieval history is one of my passions and my medievally type lifestyle and activities are sincerely done, but I'm aware that they're also a good hook for people to know me and remember me by. I'm now better known, by the public at least, for my YouTube channel Modern History TV than for Rebellion, even though I've been running the latter successfully for more than twenty-five years. Modern History TV channel gets between 3.5 million and 5 million views per month, at least double that of some exceptionally well known YouTubers, and at the time of writing this has over 650,000 subscribers. It's a bit mind-boggling to be honest; that's almost ten big sports stadia of people who have chosen to follow my personal work on video. At a US airport once they opened a new check-in station for me. I thought I was about to be detained – when you have long hair you find that officials often take a dim view of you – but no, the guy was a big fan of my YouTube channel and just wanted to talk to me. He ended up giving me a short cut route out of the crowded area! I also like the fact that YouTube videos are echoes of visual learning methods from medieval times. In general I approve of it, as it's democratised a lot things, but of course along with the great stuff there's also a lot of poorly researched or downright loony content too. Caveat emptor, as usual when you go online.

We all categorise people and think that's the sum of them. This idea of specialisation seems odd to me: people have always got several strings to their bows. Plato, for example, is famous these days as an ancient philosopher, but he was also a wrestler: in fact, Plato seems to be a nickname and means 'broad-shouldered', so was perhaps his wrestling name. Imagine Giant Haystacks crossed with Bertrand Russell, or The Rock segueing into a roundtable discussion on ethics. (The discussion would presumably be a bit different when he can suplex you.) Take Brian May, who apart from being the guitarist for Queen is also an astrophysicist of note. It's not that people are necessarily totally rounded, but certainly they may be a different shape from what you thought. Mark Taimanov was a Soviet chess grandmaster who was also a concert-standard pianist. 'When I play chess I think about music, and when I play the piano I think about chess: but I never get the two mixed up.' He always maintained that his two careers complemented each other and that he would only have lost out by favouring one over the other. 'Everything is simpler when you don't have one unique goal in your life.' Or the Hollywood actress Hedy Lamarr, who helped develop frequency-hopping spread spectrum technology, versions of which would later be used in Bluetooth and wifi.

So I like to find out what really makes people tick, what they're like behind and beyond the office persona. For my part, I spent two years doing a DPhil on the behaviour of game birds and predators after my undergraduate degree. (I never actually completed the studies or wrote the thesis up at all, so I don't get to have the Dr. bit of my name added.) In a parallel universe, perhaps another version of me did write the work up and became an eminent professor and runs a department at some university or other. I hope I enjoy the academic lifestyle. In the end I embraced another life, that of storytelling and computer games within a field of ever advancing, ever changing technology, as my passion was as much creativity as hard science. I drifted away from academia rather than having an epiphany or anything. Business meant travel, people, expansion, changes and money: even though I'm not especially materialistic, I knew I needed funds to come in to keep growing the business successfully.

I competed in modern pentathlon at Oxford as well as playing hockey for St John's and riding for the University in competitions. Modern pentathlon is one of those multi-sports, like decathlon, but rather than ten it involves five specialist disciplines – riding, shooting, swimming, fencing and running. It is based on the skills a Victorian cavalry officer would have needed to fight and if necessary I assume escape from behind enemy lines. I rode very well, easily up to Olympic standard, I shot well and was fit enough to run fast. But swimming and fencing were hard. Swimming because it was difficult to find the time and facilities to train enough and fencing was another skill entirely, so my qualifications for this sport were very lopsided. I worked hard on the fencing part and managed a little swimming, but swimming in particular was my Achilles heel. How much any of this would directly feed into my work is impossible to say, but it's all part of me and therefore part of what I bring to the company, and the physical fitness and riding and to a great extent the fencing, though with medieval longswords, not the sporting epee, has stayed with me for years.

Different people bring different things to the table in a business, and even when people have the same job title and/ or similar experience it's entirely possible that they might have different skills. A good team member, like a good squire, has lots of acquired knowledge about how things work which is hard to write down or even accurately quantify, but it's clear it has a lot of value. I prefer to focus on outcomes rather than titles, and I don't want my co-workers slotted into a cubicle either literally or metaphorically. I dislike cubicle culture. Yes, people need their own space in which to concentrate, but an open plan office encourages communication and co-operation, I find.

Chapter Nine

Liberality

FOR THE MEDIEVAL knight, the quality of liberality was synonymous with generosity and largesse. This was not just about giving away money or material possessions, but something wider. The French theologian and poet Alain de Lille (the original name sounds altogether more stylish than 'Alan of Lille') said that '*largitas* [the Latin term for 'liberality' or 'largesse'] in a man caused him to set no store on greed or gifts, and to have nothing but contempt for bribes'. However, we've covered much of the importance of charity and lack of excess materialism in previous chapters, so for 'liberality' these days I'd like to recast slightly. For me, liberality is an openness of mind which is crucial in today's world, and in the area of computer gaming no less than elsewhere. Openness leads to discovery, and discovery is crucial not just in our business but in every creative sector. Ideas can come from anywhere: from things you read, things you see, conversations you have, and even from your competitors. I play other people's games in my spare time so I can consume their productivity, and pay for the privilege too.

Access to market in computer games these days is relatively straightforward now. It certainly didn't used to be with gate keepers limiting access to your audience. (Weirdly this gatekeeping process still happens in film and TV, which are much older media than games, but seem to have stagnated in their business forms.) Discovery – getting people to hear about your great game – is hugely important. So I'd say getting your game developed and finished is only the first part: getting people to know about it is just as important. There's no point having a great game if no-one plays it. It used to be that shop managers would curate choices for you as their shelf space was physically limited, so they would choose which games, books, films and music you might like. Now there's no limit to the length of digital shelves, which means that retail's historic division of content into frontlist and backlist (frontlist being a content provider's newest stuff, backlist being older) is mostly meaningless. If you discover something for the first time then it's new to you no matter how old it is (within reason of course, assuming it's in a language you can understand; obviously there are old books written in older forms of English or other languages that are hard to understand). So nowadays discovery comes down to algorithms. Big lumps of code and data that determine what you might be offered and what the system thinks you will like the best. The science of why people make decisions is vital: modern-day algorithms check even the slightest discrepancy in habits and work to understand and take advantage of those variations. They in summary compare your behaviour with other people's behaviours and map one onto the other to guess that you'll like the same thing. Sometimes this goes very wrong. I once purchased a chainsaw on Amazon and was offered another chainsaw afterwards. Only quite rarely does one need to buy two chainsaws in one day.

This is the challenge for every game developer or creator of content: how do we make a title attract people? How do we get players to commit hours of their lives to playing one of our computer games? We generally make titles for an audience that many would describe as the hardcore gamer. They are typically (but definitely not exclusively) male and in their mid-twenties to mid-forties, though with the rapidly changing nature of our audience that description is getting a little creaky these days. And there's a lot of competition for anybody's time: not just other games but screen time in general. When a brilliant action adventure show appears on television, for example, we can sometimes see a slight drop in our player statistics or sales because people are attracted away by the new shiny show. Television can have the opposite effect too, of course: sales of our *Nazi Zombie Army* game soared when *The Walking Dead* first appeared on British screens in 2010.

Consumers come in all shapes and sizes, as do their habits. There are those who get very fixated on one thing, and those who dabble in several things. This kind of coexistence of breadth and depth is key to our understanding of our consumers. I want as many people as possible to discover and play our games. But discovery is also a competitive thing. Everybody's trying to make good stuff, and most people's stuff is pretty good. People have only got a certain number of spare hours to spend. If they play the *Sniper Elite* games they'll enjoy them, almost certainly. But can we persuade them to have a go? The answer is yes we can, in lots of different ways. I want our games to be available on every platform possible (a platform is games industry jargon for 'type of computer', like an Xbox or a Playstation), because we think the challenge is discovery, so we're not that bothered what flavour of platform our games are on. Ideally they're on them all.

What we care about is: can people get to play games wherever they are on the globe? We try to sell our games everywhere in the world, wherever they have data connectivity. We can earn income from Chinese consumers, which is relatively unusual for some industries: it's normally Chinese businesses getting money from non-Chinese consumers. In emerging markets, as people become more middle-class and have disposable income, and spare time, one of the things we hope they will want to do is play computer games. That's very exciting, and it's a lovely way to have soft power and soft influence over the globe. If people are playing our computer games, then hopefully they think well of us.

On Steam, which is one of the biggest digital markets for games on the PC platform, people have said our season passes, the extra content we make after making the main game, are some of the best value ones they've seen. And that's brilliant, that tells me that we've done the right thing for players. Word gets around in a virtuous cycle. We want to entertain them, we want them to feel that they've got their money's worth. Because it's nice to entertain others with your work and more pragmatically we want them to come back and play the next game. That's an important thing: the repeat business. So if somebody plays one of our games we want them to say, 'I've really enjoyed that. What's next from them? What have they got in their back catalogue that I can buy?' Indeed, projecting forward I think we'll soon lose intermediaries when it comes to media. In the medium term I think it unlikely we will be paying a monthly subscription to any walled garden service such as Netflix which includes a whole lot of stuff we never consume: we'll pay for and watch only what we want and pay for those individually. You'll simply say something human: 'I'd like to watch a science fiction show please' and the assistant, a sophisticated AI, will make some suggestions to you based on vast amounts of data and what it thinks you'll like. You'll make the final choice, and the owner of the rights will get paid, but it'll be transparent to you the consumer. The two fixed points in the system are the creator and the consumer: all other parts are fungible. It's like when we make a phone call: I don't know who carries the call, who gets what money, when or how, and I don't care, I just want the connection to be clear and stable. I have my phone on a specific network that I pay a regular amount for, but obviously the phone can connect to lots of other networks transparently to me, and presumably everybody involved gets a tiny cut of the money.

Some companies have signed their game titles up for exclusive deals on one platform or another. We've generally (with one exception so far) steered away from this methodology, as in an ideal world I want as many people as possible to be able to buy our games on whatever their favourite game platform might be. However I can see that this is likely to change in the future as exclusive content can help build up an audience. Generally, no-one complains when a TV show or movie is exclusively on one system or channel after all; in fact the whole of the film and TV industry is nothing but exclusives. (I'm not sure anything non-exclusive even exists there.) The games industry has developed quite differently, with wide availability on as many platforms and electronic 'shop windows' as possible being the norm. Exclusives are relatively unusual, unless they're fully funded by one platform holder or another, and then usually positioned as a 'platform seller'. For me the relationship I have with the consumer is important, and it matters to me how many people buy and play our games. We listen to our fans as best we can. Somebody buying an exclusive game from us is not just compensating us for lost sales on the other platform X or Y. It does usually de-risk a project somewhat in that you have a guaranteed income, but you also have to factor in the cost of the negative reaction from people who are upset by the decision not to have a game they want on their system of choice. People can kick up quite a fuss sometimes on social media. There's also a fairness aspect to this, and I want to be fair to the fans who want to buy it on the platform they want.

But we *have* done exclusives once in a while, when it made good business sense. We did a year's exclusive deal with Epic for *Zombie Army 4*. Epic paid a fair price to compensate us for not having the game on other systems. *Zombie Army 4* was one of those games they wanted that they felt would drive consumers to their new distribution service. Sometimes, as an independent developer, you've got to take your chances. When something like that is offered, and you think the upside is sufficient to balance the downside, then you do that sort of deal. You end up sharing both the risk and the reward.

Epic were disrupting the existing market. Steam had been the main contender on the PC platform, with a huge and impressive market share. That kick up the backside whenever a new competitor comes into the marketplace tends to energise everyone. Many people in the industry think that the huge success of PlayStation 2 was directly responsible for the arguably underwhelming launch of the PlayStation 3, as too much complacency had crept in, and Sony rested on their laurels. (I find it amusing that there's even a phrase from antiquity like 'resting on one's laurels' so it's not as if the phenomenon is limited to the games industry.)

Discovery works on many different fronts. For example, I enjoy the process of helping children think about the past as if it were today rather than something 'other' that happens on the screen. Some years ago, I was in my medieval knight's armour with Warlord resident in a real medieval castle in Wales (or more properly Cymru) for the weekend. Actually sleeping and cooking in a medieval pavilion tent and going about knightly things during the day. It was a properly immersive adventure for me, and something I would like to do more of one day. The place was visited by bands of feral school children, who were excitedly running around the place, climbing where they were not wanted and asking chaotically worded but enthusiastic questions. Some are cheeky little buggers, but you can almost see their brains working: 'Wow, I've met someone wearing real armour.' It was there that I showed them that a knight in full plate harness can get on his horse from the ground unaided. I did it several times in spite of which the teacher insisted that they couldn't. I hope the kids learned that a teacher can be wrong and that sometimes what people tell us needs to be carefully considered and not just believed. I have occasionally been on the receiving end of people wondering why I do what I do and take it so seriously. In my defence, should it even be necessary to defend what you enjoy doing, I think games and hobbies are important to many people, in terms of entertaining them, being a distraction and making them happy. It's a valuable thing for society to have happier people, but it's nice to do educational things too, preferably educational without being unentertaining. I find I learn well when I'm interested, engaged and enjoying myself.

Sometimes Rebellion does things that at the time observers and commentators speculate has no value. So far they've always been very wrong indeed. In 2016 we acquired within a vast comics library dating back over a century a character that is world famous, *Roy of the Rovers*, so that an entire new generation could discover him. Nostalgia's great, but nostalgia is our past, and we wanted to be creating new nostalgia for the generations after us. So, as with all our acquisitions of older intellectual property, it isn't a case of just re-releasing the old, original stuff that's valuable and hard to find, but also reimagining and relaunching him as a young man at the beginning of his footballing career. Comics are quite a good place to help encourage reluctant readers, and part of our thinking was using *Roy of the Rovers* to encourage people to read more. Reluctant readers are predominantly underprivileged boys, and footy is something that is socially acceptable for them to read and talk about. They're more comfortable with it as a subject, they understand football, so can engage with the story tropes and ideas, and they can see the pictures and the more difficult words often have clues in the pictures to help understanding.

Talking of education, I've got a friend whose kid is a big fan of *Sniper Elite*. He was saying that one of the unintended consequences of his son playing our *Sniper Elite* games, with their infamous gory bullet camera sequences, was that they both knew human anatomy really well. They'd play together and his son would ask, 'Dad, what's that I've just shot?' and he'd reply, 'I don't know, I'll have to go look it up. Oh, that's the liver.' This dad said that the game had given his son a fairly expert knowledge of human insides, which is bizarre if you think about it. Obviously shooting the testicles ended in hoots of laughter, you know – it's a fifteen-year-old's gameplay style – but it's an interesting outcome of accurate entertainment forms. I'm not saying it's an educational game, but it has those unintended consequences. You learn where somebody's spleen is, you see where the lungs are and where the heart is. Maybe you haven't done biology at school yet, you might not know, and bizarrely enough a game like this would show you. It really isn't for under 18s, but it was interesting feedback. I hadn't expected anybody to learn anatomy through *Sniper Elite*.

Of course, I pointed out that technically you're not meant to give the game to your fifteen-year-old, that it's an 18 certificate, and designed for an adult audience, and clearly labelled as such, but he was okay with his son playing. He's the dad, it's his job, but though it does say 18 on the box playing the game together has helped them communicate, discuss ideas and learn. Clearly kids under the age of the game's rating ideally shouldn't be playing; however, being realistic, I do think that you can argue ultimately it's the parents' choice, and down to their judgement on the suitability of the title for their child. Different areas of the world consider different aspects of content to make a game unsuitable for those under adult age. The USA seems OK with gun violence and killing, but not with nudity, while France is happy with nudity and not with violence. Societies differ significantly. Germany, for clangingly obvious reasons, has issue with certain symbols. It will probably not come as a surprise to you these days, but the vast majority of our players are grown-ups. Our average player age is probably something like mid-thirties, so it's only one extreme end that anyone needs to be concerned about. But I guess if your son's fifteen or sixteen and you, as a responsible parent, think that this game is suitable then that's your choice. It's up to you how you raise your kids. I'm a believer in guidelines and clear labelling so people can make informed choices but if people are grown-ups then they can do what they like and if people have got their own kids, well, as long as they understand what it is they're doing then I think it's up to them. Other people might disagree and draw the line in a different place. Obviously you wouldn't want some of our games in the hands of a ten-year-old.

The question of video games and violence sometimes raises its head when I'm in conversations with the media. A clip of *Sniper Elite 4* was featured in a montage shown at the White House about video games and their connection to actual violence. Without permission I must add and without our knowledge, and I'm pretty sure it was a breach of copyright law. It was all over the international news, which was a bit of a salutary lesson because we're based in the UK, we're a UK studio, and sometimes I can forget the global reach of what we do and how influential the games business can be in contemporary society. I still think of games as a minority pursuit in some ways, a fringe industry, but it's clearly not: all the stats say it's very much an important part of people's media consumption and a much bigger industry overall than TV or movies or music. That takes some getting used to as it didn't start out that big, and many in the 'old' media still haven't fully taken that to heart. Even the government is slowly coming round to realising what an industrial powerhouse our industry really is. They still give out honours to actors, singers and TV people in vastly greater numbers than they do for the computer games industry.

The games industry itself remains oddly undiscovered not by the billions who play it but by much of the establishment. I've almost lost count of the times I've spoken to politicians, civil servants, even the BBC, and the first question I've been asked is a general, 'So, can you tell me about the games industry?' Imagine saying something similar to, say, a Premiership football player: 'So, can you tell me about professional football?' It would be inconceivably facile. It's not just that they haven't done their research, which is itself discourteous: it's that if they had done they'd have found that the games industry is incredibly successful – the biggest branch of creative industries worldwide by a large margin – which makes the issue the 800lb gorilla in the room, as it shows up their ignorance even more.

In some ways it's the kind of niche which fantasy fiction enjoyed for a while (at least until the advent of Harry Potter), overlooked by the *soi-disant* influencers but still very popular, not just through the numbers of those who consumed it but the enthusiasm with which they did too. This kind of marginalisation can also be seen in the oddity of bracketing fantasy and sci-fi together, as they're completely different genres. Perhaps the people who do think that the same people read both, with an unspoken implication that these people are not themselves ever going to be opinion formers as they're not the *bien pensant*. It's snobbery, pure and simple, and I ought to hate it, but I don't because it's funny and the joke's on them. They're missing out and they don't even know it, which is even funnier.

We take feedback from our players seriously: so seriously, in fact, that we have a whole team of staff dedicated to the players and the wider Rebellion community. We do a lot of work with social media direct to our game players. We are always trying to disintermediate, trying to get as direct to the consumer as possible. We'll always have to work with partners, and that's fine. However, we want to have as few partners taking value out of the value chain as possible, so the consumer can get something more cheaply and we can get more value from the same consumer sale.

Our business has never been better. We go as direct as we can. We want to build up our relationship with our players, and we like getting feedback from them, especially when it's constructive, but even nasty comments can be useful sometimes.

What we've tried to do, in our history, is make games that we and other people want to play. And early in our history there were a lot of people in the way that have left us completely separated from our players; sometimes the powers that be have actually physically stopped us from talking to them. In the past some publishers have said, 'Don't say anything about the game, don't engage with journalists, make no comments at all, you've got a confidentiality clause. You can't talk about it, don't do any publicity'. Whereas now we have forums, we talk directly to people; people say, 'I really love playing *Sniper Elite 4*, what else have you got coming up?' So we can directly speak to them, which is wonderful. But we can also provide better value consumer support and none of the money has to go to an entity that adds little value: instead, it goes back into feeding and keeping roofs over the heads of all the talented and skilful games making people and their families here.

In general, we don't even mind when people rant at us about games, because we learn something from that passion and that feedback. But there are limits. People's worlds are increasingly focussed around themselves, and in the digital world especially people feel entitled to get what they want and get it *now*. It doesn't matter that what they want takes a team of twenty people three months to do and has only been going a third of that time: the impatient consumer will still say, 'That's not good enough.' Once at *2000 AD* we had a letter threatening the editor with violence if a certain character didn't appear in the next issue, even though of course that issue was already at the distributors and the one after that at the printers. There's a thin line between being a very passionate fan and being rudely desperate, and I've seen that line crossed many times. Consumers occasionally misunderstand or over simplify the process of getting something to market: they discover something, enjoy it and want more, no matter that what they want involves vast amounts of work.

And the entitlement doesn't end with just access to the work: it also encompasses perceived quasi ownership of and rights to that work. Look at the furore around the finale of *Game of Thrones*, when people petitioned the showrunners to redo the entire season, and as of writing this, are still trying to get it redone. Writing anything longer than a Facebook status update, and making it good, is unbelievably hard. Multiply that many times when writing a fantasy series full of characters and complex plot lines. Multiply that many times again when having to adapt extremely long and detailed source books. Multiply that many times again when the series becomes the most successful of all time and the pressure to keep the standard up increases with every season. And multiply that many times again when everyone out there with a smartphone thinks they could do better. Just for clarity, I'm not saying it was a good ending though.

If you as a viewer were disappointed in the last season, fine. That's your right, and nothing and no-one should be immune from criticism. But if you signed a petition for HBO to reshoot that season, or said that you felt betrayed, or accused the showrunners David Benioff and D.B. Weiss of being talentless hacks, then wind your neck in. It's not just you that's invested heart and soul into the last decade of *Game of Thrones*. They have too: they, and everyone else who's worked on it, in front of or behind the camera. You've watched it and loved it and talked about it, but seventy-three episodes over all that time is only the briefest of intermissions in your life, and to pretend otherwise is the height of entitlement. For them, it has been their working life. They've given it their all, and at least respect that even if you disagree with their choices. Besides, if they hadn't done such a great job with the first seven seasons you wouldn't be upset by the eighth, would you?

Most people, in all walks of life, are just trying their best. It's easy to forget that when the natural instinct, magnified hugely by social media, is to lay into them for the slightest thing. Criticise by all means, but make it constructive and don't make it personal. One day, it might be you on the receiving end. And as Neil Gaiman said in a blogpost to those who also complained about the slow writing pace of George R.R. Martin, on whose books *Game of Thrones* is based:

> '*George R.R. Martin is not your bitch*... People are not machines. Writers and artists aren't machines... Some writers need a while to charge their batteries, and then write their books very rapidly.' (journal.neilgaiman.com, 12 May 2009)

Evelyn Waugh apparently used to have a selection of ten different pre-printed postcards which he would send to those who wrote in complaining about something or other in his books. The postcards, of course, were nothing by way of actual engagement with the letter-writer, but rather bland and deliberately passive-aggressive fob-offs ('thank you for your most edifying suggestion', etc.). Of course, in those days actually writing to the publisher was an effort – you had to find their address, write the letter, post it, and wait for a reply. Now it can all be done via e-mail or tweet in a matter of seconds, and often without direct human consequences.

I see this with my YouTube channel too. Most of the comments are positive, but inevitably there are always a few which are highly critical, abusive or pointless. I just delete the abusive ones. There's no point dealing with people like that, as they're not interested in dialogue. I wonder what they get out of it – a momentary blip of satisfaction? A cry for attention?

– but I try not to dwell on it, as that kind of negativity can really affect you badly if you let it. It's human nature to forget the ninety-nine percent of positive comments and focus on the one percent negative. Some people just get enriched by being negative. You find people who've played a game for 150 hours online and then heavily critcise it. If you've played for an hour and offer constructive criticism as to why it's not for you, fine. But not if you've played for the best part of a week straight!

More generally, the pandemic will lead to new avenues of discovery in several areas, just as Middle Ages plagues did. The silk routes themselves were part of the plague history, and from those routes came much of high fashion which nobles and aristocrats adopted, along with death and disease. There are definite comparisons between COVID-19 and the 14th-century bubonic plague which ravaged Europe, not so much in the number of dead but in terms of shaking up the way people think. The Black Death really can be argued to have marked the beginning of the end of the Middle Ages and the birth of events that would become what we know in hindsight as the Renaissance – one of the first Renaissance novels, Giovanni Boccaccio's *Decameron*, is a selection of stories told by ten friends in Florence as they shelter from the plague. The human response to danger and trauma on a grand scale has always been to think in a new way, if only because it takes such seismic levels of shock to persuade those with a vested interest in the status quo as it was that things need to change and that old paradigms are no longer sufficient. Pandemics have been accelerators of mental renewal: when you're in a whirlwind you have to think anew.

Indeed, plenty of places ravaged by the Black Death bounced back stronger than ever, though over decades, not weeks. In Italy, for example, as in many places, there were so few workers left that labour was scarce, which in turn meant that wages rose, which in turn meant that artisans and labourers became more powerful, not just economically but politically and socially too. The relative standing of capital and labour, which had been tipped very much towards capital, was now reversed. Falling food prices and rising wages both hit the landed gentry hard, former serfs became wealthier, and women (many of them widows) found employment and empowerment in depopulated professions that had been male dominated previously.

The same kind of disruption to the established order can be seen with Covid. For example, Zoom meetings have become an accepted part of the business landscape with a speed and reach they would never have managed without the pandemic: necessity, in this case, being very much the mother of invention. In turn they have prompted people to reassess the need and desirability of endless international travel. Why spend all that money on flights, hotels and dinners when you can do so much – though not all – of that through a computer screen? Even the conversations we had for this book, a dozen sessions of two hours each, were all done on Zoom and didn't suffer in any way from not being done in person. This may well be part of a revolution of both communications and infrastructure: change which in hindsight will seem inevitable, as for example the smoking ban did, but which was very much not so at the time. The logic for spending billions on HS2 to shave twenty minutes off the trip from London to Birmingham becomes very shaky when ninety percent of the meetings which HS2 would have facilitated can be done without either party leaving home. One salutary lesson for me is that we used to travel to London for a board meeting of a trade body of which I'm the co-founder and chair, TIGA. Those meetings took two hours, but probably two hours for me to get there, and two hours for the return journey. A whole working day more or less. In the pandemic we still had the meetings but via video, and the meetings took the two hours as usual, but, and here's the interesting thing, they have all been better attended than those requiring an in-person event. It's so much easier and less costly in all ways to book two hours out of your day than a whole day. Why would we return to the in-person event now?

The pandemic has shown up the limits of planning and forecasting: to quote the late Donald Rumsfeld, 'there are known knowns, known unknowns and unknown unknowns'. The effects can be positive or negative depending on the sector you're in. Consumption of computer games, books and Netflix were all up: travel, on the other hand, was absolutely hammered. Who would have airline stocks in a black swan pandemic?

Pandemics also shine a light on the parts of society which the ruling class – which is to say not just the government but those in positions of power more generally: bankers, journalists, lawyers, officials – usually like to ignore. Covid has affected the poor more than the rich, blue-collar workers more than white-collar ones, people of colour more than whites, and so on. It has shown up the limitations of both the government and the entire socio-political structure. This, too, is liberality: the discovery of what has always been there waiting to be found and seen. Whether or not society chooses to do something with this new-found knowledge remains to be seen. Of course the opposite is also visible, with increasing amounts of anti-scientific thinking on display both in the UK and the USA: people determined not to follow the science, or to think that half an hour going down the rabbit hole of YouTube conspiracy theory videos makes them expert virologists. (For similar reasons I carefully curate my Twitter experience as far as possible: it can be a dreadful, toxic, unfiltered place, full of bots and bad actors trying to spread discontent and distrusting authority of any description.) In the age of reason, unreason is very far from dead.

Chapter Ten

Diligence

WHEN IT COMES to diligence in my business, the alpha and omega is surely the hard work involved in developing a game (and by developing it I mean going from an idea to a finished playable game), which in turn begs the question: how do you actually make a good computer game?

The first and biggest challenge is actually getting the damn thing finished, which is more difficult than it sounds. Making a game is ferociously complicated, one of the most complicated things you can do. NASA did some analysis and concluded that one of the most complicated processes done by humans – including moon shots and manned space missions – is making computer games, because of all the moving parts. And you're not doing this in a vacuum either. You can always spend an extra month or two or three or six on a game to make it even better, but you've got to make a game that fits with the budget and fits with the sales expectations so you can go on to make another one. Creative compromise is key.

The second challenge is to make a game that's good, preferably very good indeed. You can make a computer game, you can have it whirling away on screen, and it's just not fun. Trying to write down and quantify what makes a game playable is quite difficult. Why is this part of that game fun? It almost goes beyond language sometimes, and that makes it quite difficult to pin down. I'll look at gameplay, world building, narrative, graphics and so on in the course of this chapter, and they're all important in one way or another, but they're not the heart of what makes a good game. There are plenty of games out there that are really fun, that have lasted a long time, that have lousy graphics by modern standards of the art. And the same with narrative. I'm often asked to talk about narrative in games, and narrative can be an important component of games, but it doesn't have to be. A good story can be part of a game, but there are plenty of games that don't have a good story or the story is just you, the protagonist, having an adventure, and the narrative is what you make of it. I've played plenty of 'strong narrative' games in which I've simply forgotten the main story and have just played out my own tale.

I think that when creating a game, it has to come from the heart. Yes, of course we look at demographics and target markets and all that, but deep down we only make games we want to make, and which we enjoy playing. It sounds a cliché, but like all clichés it's only so because it's true: unless you make a game because you want to, it won't be truly and properly good. If you look at an existing game, see that it's successful and think 'oh, I'll have a piece of that', people will be able to tell. Learning from other people's creativity is very different to copying it. Anyone who's played enough games can tell when the development team has put heart and soul into it or when they've just lazily duplicated something that's doing well. When you do something from the heart, you do it from the inside out: a first, original creative idea which is then built upon in layers and layers to form the finished game. When you do something just for the money, you do it from the outside in, the surface appearance first, and you never get to the soul at the heart of it. Someone who plays your game for any length of time will soon realise this. So you never start out thinking something is going to be a huge success. *Sniper Elite* – and I'll use this as an example quite often in this chapter as it's one of our signature games – is right up there with titles like *Assassin's Creed* or *Call of Duty*, each billion-dollar franchises that drive multinational corporations to lofty success. OK maybe we're not quite that big, but we're in the same league. They sell three times as much as us, but they cost twenty times as much to make.

The *sine qua non* for me is that any game must be fun and rewarding. I want the player to be so immersed that they're in a state of flow: energised, totally focussed, performing actions almost without conscious thought, and so in tune with the game that they totally lose track of time and find when they finish that many more hours have passed than they thought possible. And they have to be able to do this every time they play. A game which players only want to play once is no game at all in my opinion. As with a good film or book, each time you go back to it, it should be as rewarding as the first, but unlike a book or a film, a game can take any number of different courses each time it's played.

I completed *Fallout 4* recently and I was talking to someone about it, and he said: 'Did you do the thing at the end?' And I realised I'd completely forgotten what I was supposed to be doing. You're supposed to be searching for your son, which should drive your every waking moment, but I forgot and just explored. I wasn't made to care enough at the beginning of the game, nor was I reminded about it sufficiently to really care. I was driven by the landscape to just want to go off and travel. The problem most games can't easily accept is that there's no storytelling medium that would ever try to sustain itself over 80+ hours. It's an impossible task. But that's almost the appeal of games I think, in that you can lose yourself in them. They often don't need a complex story as well. I mean, virtual reality I think is a really interesting medium because you're even more bound into it, you're literally inside the screen. But it takes effort, too. To play a good virtual reality game for any length of time is quite exhausting.

People talk about gameplay a lot and it's one of those words that means different things to different people at different times. It covers a multitude of areas, but however you choose to define it, it's absolutely critical. The 'play' part reflects the crucial aspect of any game: that this is an interactive, transitive activity. Books, movies and TV shows are passively consumed, no matter how involved with them we get: we're presented with stories and arcs predetermined by the content creators and there's nothing we can do to change them. But in a computer game the player has much more control in shaping their destiny, and the ways in which that control can be exerted is crucial. It has to be easy, natural, and rewarding: even minor inconveniences become exponentially more annoying when repeated and encountered over and over again. The game's core mechanic, the action that the player performs most often in a game, must never pall: it must be as fun to do the thousandth time as it is the first time.

For example, *Sniper Elite* can be fairly simple in terms of its core objectives: locate some hidden intelligence, destroy a strategic position, assassinate an enemy officer – but these objectives are not only clear but speak to the part of the human brain and experience which value not just these things in themselves but a person's value in doing so. Samuel Johnson said that 'every man thinks meanly of himself for not having been a soldier', and there's a certain truth in that: by extension, therefore, this is partly why so many people like to play war games as the next best thing and/or an exciting but safely ersatz version of the real thing.

There's something very satisfying about the process of taking a sniper shot. It's a three-stage process. First, find the right vantage point, with plenty of cover and clear sightlines. Second, take the shot itself: take aim, work out the variables (wind speed, air pressure, elevation drop and so on), and fire between breaths and heartbeats. Finally, move quickly and safely from the position before the enemy can find you. And because it's so satisfying, players will happily do it again and again and again.

Any good game has to be challenging. It sounds obvious, perhaps, but it can't be said too often. There needs to be threat and consequence: threats to the player's progress, consequences if they fail the task in front of them. Gamers play games in the expectation of being challenged, repeatedly and often, but not defeated. They want to have to go above themselves to complete a level: they need to work for it, or else there'll be no feeling of meaningful accomplishment. The challenge can be physical, testing a player's dexterity and co-ordination, or it can be mental: strategy, lateral thinking, searching for a hidden answer. Again with *Sniper Elite*, you can enjoy it as a challenging sniper sim or as the kind of pulp-fiction World War II action game where it's almost more fun when things go wrong. This was intentional. I don't want people restarting a level if it goes wrong. I want them to be able to recover and go 'oh, no, how am I going to keep going?' rather than go, 'well, I'd better just reload'. I don't want people to be thinking in terms of how the games designer or the level designer wanted them to play: I want them to play the game the way they want and have a living environment that responds and reacts to them in a semi-intelligent way.

We have quality assurance team members (they used to be called game testers, but the job goes way beyond 'playing games as a job') whose role it is to play games as if they were an ordinary player. In a way, role playing the playing as someone new to the game. This is hard to do when your job means you're a full-time game player so unusually good at most games; you're an actual game-playing professional. You need to find hard mode relatively easy, as the game difficulty has to scale for people who haven't had that experience, and if you can't have a chat, drink a cup of tea and play the game on easy mode at the same time, it's far too hard. Then we get others who are new to our particular game, have never seen it before to play it through, and the designers are supposed to avoid directly communicating with them as they play. 'No, no, don't go that way, go the other. Yes, press that button on the left,' etc. They can obviously take notes but can't speak until the end. The game has to speak for itself. If the designer's frustrated that the player has done the 'wrong thing', then it's their problem to work it out.

When attempting to balance a game for difficulty there are many complex and subtle ways of achieving it, without the obvious 'make the enemies harder'. For example you can up the difficulty levels by removing things from the player, rather than including them. Often there are settings in a game that act to assist novice or inexperienced players, and help them along invisibly, without making them feel like they're being helped. In the tougher settings on *Sniper Elite* we take away some of the things which help the player, such as elements of the head-up display, bullet markers to show you where the bullet may hit, and indications that the enemy know you're around. We also give different options to prevent it from being too repetitive: you as the sniper can be stealthy and unseen, but you can also use traps to lure the enemy out or just go full firefight as an all-out action game. And in terms of multiplayer mode, you can either team up with someone – there's great satisfaction in working as a two-man team, covering each other and taking out the enemy between you – or play against them and see who can score the most kills.

I like to think of a game in terms of complexity (or width) and depth, which are not the same thing. Complexity is how difficult a player finds it to learn the rules: depth is how many decisions a player has to make during the game, and how challenging and important those decisions are. A game that's too hard to learn will put players off: a game that's easy to master will leave them dissatisfied and be labelled shallow. Ideally gameplay should be easy to learn but hard to master, like *Tetris* or drumming, or most sports. This can mean having low complexity and great depth, but it doesn't always work that way. Complexity can be gradually introduced, as can depth, and sometimes that very reveal of more can keep a player going towards the end of the game. Chess is also a good example of low(ish) complexity but astounding depth: it arguably takes ten minutes to learn the rules, but the richness of possible play means that even the greatest players in history are still a long, long way off having in any way conquered the game (as can be seen by the fact that computer players are substantially stronger than even the world champion).

Rules should be easy to understand. If they're not, then two things are imperative: to introduce them gradually as the game progresses rather than info dump them all on the player to start with, as that just increases the chances the players will give up early and neither complete nor enjoy the game; and ensure that the players feel that those rules are there for a reason and that the players have the chance to influence the course of the game. Rules should generally follow their own internal logic. Making things up is fine, but you need to have a certain consistency to the way you make things up for believability. If magic works this way for one character, it should do so the same for another, unless there is some logical reason why it doesn't that's part of the game world. The ideal type of rules system to avoid is that of the radio game 'Mornington Crescent', a fascinatingly complex game, but one with almost unbelievable levels of complexity.

In general, I try to keep rules as simple as possible. There's a reason that football – or soccer, if you're from the USA – is the most popular game in the world, and that's because it's so simple and there are relatively few rules. Getting the balance right is easier said than done: even if something appears very hard to begin with, it must also feel that it can be conquered with enough time, practice and skill. The payoffs between challenge and reward are absolutely crucial, and they are never static: difficulties must escalate the longer the game goes on and the higher the level achieved. Goals are a moveable feast: there are always more to come, but never so many at once as to be overwhelming or so few at once as to be boring. The outcome – win or lose – must always be in the balance, and always down to the player's skill. Any kind of *deus ex machina*, whether to help or hinder the player, risks leaving them feeling cheated. In game design we often talk about the difficulty curve, and that's a good way of describing it. Is the slope too steep to begin with, is it undulating so gets easier then harder then easier? Are there cliffs of insane difficulty that almost no-one can climb, or troughs of ease that make it boring?

Control means that the player must never feel they're being 'played' by the game rather than vice versa; the enemies must not obviously cheat. Controls, the way in which a player gives game input, are a huge part of what makes a good game. The controls are literally the interface between player and game, so the more natural, instinctive and ergonomic you can make them the better. A well-designed controller is a work of art in itself, almost an extension of the player's nervous system, and the control system must 'feel right'. Building game input takes a lot of trial and error.

Story is also vital to some types of game (but not all); a propulsive narrative which keeps the player moving forward both literally and metaphorically can be important in open world games or role playing games in particular. One of the great things about storytelling is that the fundamentals are the same no matter the medium: characters which engage, clearly defined and worthwhile goals, twists and turns to prevent staleness and increase the stakes, and so on. As in every narrative, it's most effective to vary the pace. Going flat out the whole way is exhausting and will just burn the player out quicker. People talk about taking the player on a rollercoaster, but remember that rollercoaster designers deliberately build in lulls as well as fast bits. They don't just whirl the riders around at 100mph from start to finish: they know the need for recovery from the last big section and anticipation for the next one. Having said that there are fairground rides that do indeed just seem to whirl people around for two minutes, but if you look at them, the early parts of the ride are often the things that generate the adrenaline. Anticipation and foreshadowing are quite important elements in storytelling and fairground rides alike.

Any good game is its own world. One of the reasons I'm interested in medieval history is that it's such a richly realised and enticing world. We think we know a lot about it, but we also don't know quite a lot too, so there are things to discover and uncover, elements to reassess in light of new discoveries. I love the little details which say so much about the time: the specific design of shields and how they are strapped for different tasks, what people ate (the meat from oysters was almost a by-product of the lime industry so they were a super cheap food close to the coast), the way the different classes interacted, how they lit their home after dark. This kind of world is crucial to a good video game – not the specific medieval setting, of course, but the combination of details and attraction. If you have a science fiction world, how does it work, where does the power come from, how good are computers, do people use money? World building is at the heart of every good fantasy story, and what are video games but fantasies in their own way? Again, I don't mean this literally in terms of sword and sorcery, but metaphorically. A good game should not just take the player to another world but immerse them there, keep them there and make them extremely reluctant to return. The Mappa Mundi, which had Jerusalem at the centre, was not so much a map as a picture, a representation. If it was a map, it was a mind map. The medieval mind didn't think of myth and legend as secret or distinct from reality. I like to take some of that into our designs.

We worked very hard on the world building for *Sniper Elite 3*. The Italian landscape we chose gave us many different options for landscapes and locations: quiet Tuscan villages, vineyards, dockyards, forests, hilltop monasteries and so on. We overlaid these with the war-built environment, concrete bunkers, secret bases, hidden installations. All these are visually rewarding in their own way – even the dockyards – and so we set about immersing the player in that world: blazing heat, brave partisans, and of course the go-to villains not just of our time but of all time in the Nazis. In *Sniper Elite 4* we added to the world's accessibility and openness, allowing the player myriad ways of approaching the targets and particularly using the vertical dimension in terms of crossing rooftops, using mountain paths and finding other elevated points from where to take on the enemy.

The world isn't just visual: it's social and legal too. It's based in the real world, so it has real world consequences and decisions. For example, you can't kill civilians in *Sniper Elite*. Everyone's a combatant and everyone's armed. We even looked at the Geneva Convention for the rules about surrender. We have conversations with the team about this sort of thing all the time. We are making games based in the historical landscape, geographically as well as politically, so we deal with issues such as the activities of partisans and the resistance, underground aspects of an invaded country. We necessarily touch on fascism and Nazism in the game without being heavy-handed.

Good visuals for the sort of games we are making are crucial, which means good graphics are essential and take a lot of the time and budget to get right. Audio in computer games is getting better and better, and done well, sound will improve graphics. Most games we make are strong visual experiences: the word 'video', after all, is Latin for 'I see'. Technology now allows developers to make the graphics hyper-realistic, a trend which will only continue with the next generation of virtual reality. Great graphics on their own can't save an otherwise mediocre game. And though that technology can be hyper-realistic, it doesn't have to be. Graphics are at heart a part of art, and great art is not confined to one style: great graphics can be cartoonish, surreal, fantastical, monochrome, and so much more. *Minecraft*, for example, has very unrealistic graphics, and by any rational standards fairly low-quality ones too: but the game's look is unique and cohesive, and that's enough for its massive audience. In some ways it may even be an advantage, in that everybody's work in the game doesn't look very good so even if you are visually incapable, it doesn't matter, everybody is forced to be that way, every bit of work is levelled down.

Ask any *Sniper Elite* player about the game's graphics, and chances are they'll talk about the killcam, which shows in slow motion skulls exploding, spines shattering, intestines and organs spewing out in sprays of red. They're very gruesome but also incredibly popular – and, I would argue, educational not just in the anatomical sense of the previous chapter's discussion about a teenager learning biology, but also in the more general sense of this is what war is really like, far from the censored and sanitised images in mainstream TV drama. We had, and have, lots of discussion in-house about how far to take the killcam and what it was there for. With the killcam becoming more detailed with the muscular system and the circulatory system, we always knew where the line was, we knew where it becomes obscene. It's still diagrammatic, so we haven't gone down the slasher/gore route. It's gruesome because you're seeing what the bullet does, but it's still quite stylised. There's blood and guts, but we don't have buckets of the stuff flying all over the screen. There's a bit of it but I think we've made it appropriately horrible as opposed to inappropriately horrible.

Obviously, for lots of people it's the payoff, it's the reward for taking the shot. But it's an interesting one because we weren't really doing it to glorify killing; just the exact opposite. There's no question that it's entertaining for many people, but a lot of people find it horrific, which is exactly the point because sniping is one of those weird things in war. From reading memoirs and talking to people, it's clear that snipers are in a fairly unique position in that they're slightly feared by the soldiers on their own side because of what they do. There's a 'them and us' kind of feeling that a lot of memoirs talk about. Snipers would sit alone in the mess tent. So we wanted to emphasise to the adult player – because it's very definitely an adult game – the nature of what one bullet can do. It's interesting how people react to it, because for some people it's the awful realisation that 'oh god… that's what happens'. And it makes them not want to shoot everybody: they only shoot the people they have to shoot in order to complete the mission. And that's part of it really, because we've tried to design our missions so that it isn't about killing every possible enemy, it isn't just shooting all the pop-up targets, it's about making key decisions about who to kill, which is even more horrible if you think about it enough.

Every shot should trouble the player on some level. I find it easier to shoot lots and lots of zombies and not worry in the slightest because they're already dead. But *Sniper Elite* is immersive in a different way, it's entertaining in a different way. There are some movies that are quite troubling, and those are entertaining in a different way. I'm hoping that we've made a fairly sophisticated piece of adult entertainment. In *Sniper Elite 4*, you might have one German guard where the intel says he has two young children, and he's really looking forward to going home, and the other guard might be torturing partisans to death and is a well-known bully, so you become more comfortable with taking that one out. There are these layers of gameplay for an older, more sophisticated audience.

We hope people don't see the killcam as gratuitous. You can turn it off in the menus. I insisted that there's a 'killcam off' toggle, because some people just don't want to see it. I don't blame them, sometimes it is quite shocking. Some people find that it breaks the game flow for them, others find it cathartic; a few just revel in it and want lots of gore in their entertainment. We need to make it scaleable for the audience and accommodate different play styles and different themes of visual entertainment.

Sound design is critical. Good, strong, resonant sounds can make such a difference: when you hear a really good rendering of a rifle shot or an active reload, it stirs a visceral reaction inside you. For *Sniper Elite* we worked hard on the sound design, not just with the gunshots but also the other sounds which snipers can use to mask their shots – planes passing overhead, artillery fire, explosions in other parts of the gamescape, that kind of thing. We did record the real sounds of all the weapons, but you won't be surprised when I say that the real sounds are not as 'good' as the built sounds the sound designers have put together. Actual gunfire sounds very much like fireworks, which must be a huge source of problem for those suffering from PTSD.

Strange Brigade is a good example of a game where all these things came together. The Strange Brigade is an international group of elite adventurers blessed with the ability to call upon the supernatural, and for this game we sent them to North Africa where Seteki the Witch Queen has risen from the dead, ready to resurrect an evil empire erased from the history books. So we made it a bit fun, a bit scary, and very much a kind of adventure that harks back to things like Saturday matinee movies, the *Boy's Own* comics, and so on. We wanted a really fantastical, fun story for players to revel in and we wanted the horror to be what I suggested should be called dry gore rather than wet gore. Mummies are after all desiccated corpses, so shooting them just turns them into dry fragments.

We came up with lots of different characters, but in the end, we focussed down on four characters that we felt were balanced and played the best of all the characters that we came up with. They make a fine group of 1930s almost-superheroes, especially with their supernatural amulet powers, and of course we knew we could add more characters in later iterations of the game.

In terms of adjusting combat to make it feel just right, like anything to do with gameplay it's about feel, so it was an iterative process. The team makes an educated guess as to the right controls and then others play the game as much as they can, give feedback, and then you re-think, 'Actually, if it was slightly different this way, maybe it would be better.' We keep redoing and modifying it until it feels just right, until the game has a wonderful mix of variety, tension and challenge, all very carefully balanced, but quite subjective too. For example, we were very keen to include environmental traps which could be used against enemies, and they're great because they're bullet savers. But they also can be occasionally activated, either accidentally or deliberately, and used against your fellow players. We felt they added quite a good flavour to the environments. They can be used very strategically and good players will use them well. But they're also just fun. You can really muck around with them: in our game, death isn't permanent.

We do have some puzzles that you'll be required to complete to open up a chamber or unearth a secret tomb, but there are many, many puzzles that are optional for those who like to explore a bit more. We reward those more explorer-type players with lots of glittering goodies – treasure, relics, and lots of ways to improve your weaponry and unlock new supernatural powers.

People talk about *Indiana Jones* being a reference point for us in the game, and they're partially correct, but also wrong. We went back a lot further than that, to the references that the writers of Mr. Jones's adventures drew inspiration from. The *Indiana Jones* movies, in tone and content, are basically very high quality film versions of the much lower budget Saturday matinees of the 1930s, '40s and '50s, as remembered by the men who were boys back then. For *Strange Brigade* we went back to the same source material, including novels from around the 1920s and even Victorian pulp novels known as the penny dreadful at the time. There is no real start to the genre; it just comes in different forms. But in particular for us, we wanted to play with those ideas in a visual medium. So we come from the same place as Indiana Jones: we are going right back to basics, back to the origins of this kind of action-adventure video game. And one of the most emblematic elements of that is the narrator, who comments on some of the very tropes that germinated in those origins. He'll wonder who's meticulously lighting up all these candles in the spooky cave, who's reloading the traps: how come the ropes are still intact and the traps still work if they've been abandoned for a thousand years? Of course it doesn't matter. The conceit we have is fine. For *Strange Brigade* we're not as bound by reality as we are with, say, *Sniper Elite*.

Even the games that didn't go quite as planned, I'm proud of them. But if you said I had to pick one of my absolute favourites then I'd say *Alien vs. Predator* for the Atari Jaguar. It was our first big commercial game as Rebellion and a real landmark moment from both a business and creative perspective. We achieved a lot with it and in many ways we were ahead of our time. The game has so many innovations – things like the photogrammetric techniques to acquire the graphics, or being able to play as a 'baddie' character. You could play as an alien, a predator or a colonial marine. The alien didn't have ranged weapons, so you had to have speed and manoeuvrability – across ceilings, through vents, and up and down walls. The alien was the hardest character to play, but it was the best character if you were very good at it. It was weak unless you could sneak up and get in close: you could drop down on somebody and bite their face off.

Though the visuals seem simplistic and sparse by today's standards, back in 1994 they were the bomb. We photographed models of the alien protagonists, animated them by hand and scanned the developed photos in for further artwork. I loved it. The *Aliens* movie, as opposed to *Alien*, was the type of sci-fi that I have always liked: a type of science fiction which involves blocked toilets, oil leaks, make-do-and-mend, bad weather, all the stuff that will exist in the future, but that we happily gloss over when we want an escapist sci-fi fantasy. The feel was basically Vietnam or World War II but with futuristic weapons. Our protagonists, who aren't heroes really, but just humans in a bad place, spit, they sweat, they go to the loo, and things are trying to eat them. I like that side of things. I call it dirty or scruffy sci-fi. You'll notice that Star Trek is always clean and neat, everything in its place, everybody washed and in clean uniforms (mostly, unless they're strategically singed in a fight). It's the same with Star Wars. It looks so clean, even the bar room scenes are swept and dusted after the heroes have left. Maybe it's the horse manager in me; I'm often covered in hair, dirt and hay, let alone horse saliva and oils from their coats. There's something unrealistic about perfectly tidy landscapes. It's the same with photoshoots for magazines of people's living rooms. Everything is in its place, not a tea cup out or tatty book ready to read, no notes of ideas, nothing on the shelves, and surfaces that are sterile and empty of the normal detritus of a busy physical life. Personally I think they look like morgues, and show-case the same type of people, dead ones.

But equally one of the things I feel is important, always, is that when you're making a game based on a really great movie, what you shouldn't do is reprise the movie. You mustn't make an interactive version of the movie. What I believe you should do is to boil it down to its rich meaty core. You take the essence of what the *Aliens* franchise is, and then build it back up again as a new story. That was really what we wanted to do. We didn't want to copy the story, nor could we as games don't work like movies – they need to have gameplay in them. We wanted to create an experience.

Sometimes game ideas come out of seemingly nowhere. *Nazi Zombie Army*, for example, was originally a bit of an experiment we had. The team up in Runcorn had about three months on their schedule before they were about to come onto *Sniper Elite 3* with not much to do, so we wanted to experiment with four-player co-op as well, see if there was anything we could do, and really throw in as many AIs as possible. AI, or Artificial Intelligence, is what drives the enemies in a game, what makes them do what they do and respond to what the player is doing. Good AI takes a lot of processing to do especially if you're trying to emulate what an intelligent human soldier might do in any situation for example. So the obvious thing here, the simplest kind of AI to do is really dumb. They're a little more stupid and threatening than shambling zombies, where the zombies just try to track you down directly, but slowly, they surround and eat you. Object avoidance, or best paths to take, or tactical approaches, let alone taking cover, selecting ammo types, backing off when flanked, are irrelevant to zombies, they're just focussed on eating the contents your of skull. So we chucked an awful lot of zombies into this game, a humungous number of entities. We chucked about eighty quite high resolution creatures into a rough four-player co-op game, and it was so much fun that we just said, 'Look, guys, we've got this, can we do something with this? Can we throw a game out there as a true indie, self-funded and not much marketing, and see how it goes?'

And it went really, really well, absolutely brilliantly. I mean, the name itself was meant to be a bit of a parody, but also do what it says on the tin. Chris came up with it against a background of negative feedback from some members of the team. In our opinion the title of something needs to tell the potential purchaser exactly what they're going to be buying. Clever titles don't work well, unless you're prepared to spend a huge amount of marketing money on telling people about it. The name wasn't meant to be sophisticated or clever or artsy, it was meant to tell people it was a zombie game with Nazis in it! It's very B-movie, and that was the whole idea. We really riffed off a lot of those '70s and '80s horror movies with the John Carpenter-esque music and the synths that they used and that whole atmosphere. It takes itself very seriously in-game though it isn't a very serious topic. People loved it! The four-player co-op lends itself to YouTube videos, so we've had an awful lot of coverage on YouTube from it; a huge, huge amount, it's been really interesting. And it's really great to see people enjoying the game that we've made as well, because often we don't get to see enough people enjoying playing our work. We get to see reviews, we get a bit of feedback from quite a lot of consumers, but we don't often get to see somebody actually playing our games. It's quite fun to watch people playing it and screaming and shouting at each other, making fun of each other and screwing around and messing up, and that's been really good.

We had to change the game in Germany because of their censorship laws and their collective sensitivity to certain symbols linked to the past, especially in computer games, which many legislators seem to think were mostly played by children (they're not). We had to take all the swastikas out, and we had various German players complaining that they can't play with other people because it's technically a different game. It's exactly the same game in Germany, but we've been required by law to change the graphics. On digital platforms like Steam, for example, it has to be published as a 'different' game, so for technical reasons those with what some people call the censored versions sadly can't play with others not using the censored version. It's annoying but there's nothing we can do to fix it; the tech to do it is not in our control. We can try and change the German law I suppose. I think one day it will be changed or get softened. You're now allowed to show swastikas in movies in Germany for example, just not if it's making the Nazis out to be heroes and must be in an historical context, not a frivolous one, and I suspect that games are not considered art and are frivoles. It's just in games that 'the Wolfenstein law' still holds. No-one's re-tested that law and it's never been challenged in the courts, so we just have to follow the law as we understand it, until someone decides to spend money and attempt to change it.

Overall when it comes to making games, we have one priceless advantage. We have our own custom game engine, called Asura; it helps us remain autonomous and react speedily to any changes in the tech world. It's not that you should have to fit your game into the restrictions of an engine. It should be the other way around. When we make a game we don't have to worry about what the engine can do because what we do is we can make the engine different and better. We can say to the engine team, 'Guys, can we do this?' and they might say, 'We can do that but we'll have to lose this.' What we can do then is work the games design around it. The engine should be there to serve the games design, the vision and the storytelling. It's not that you should have to fit your game into the restrictions of an engine. It should be the other way around. The engine should serve the gameplay experience in its greater glory. It's never been a deliberate policy. It's where we've started and never stopped.

Chapter Eleven

Hope

THE SPANISH KNIGHT Sir Ramon Llull said, 'Hope is the primary instrument of chivalry, like the hammer is the primary instrument of the carpenter.' Whilst we can argue that maybe an axe or a saw is also essential, or even a decent chisel, the medieval knight understood that hope – optimism, positiveness, good cheer, even inspiration – was not an optional extra but a vital part of his character. The belief that human life is progress, that tomorrow will be a better day than today, is one of the most vital psychological tools we have. If a leader doesn't feel that, however, why on earth should anyone else?

Hope is part of the human condition. It's easy to dismiss the hope with which medieval pilgrims set out as simply a product of their superstition, but people still go to Lourdes in their thousands, or walk the same mountainous pilgrimage routes of Saint Iago de Compostela as they did in medieval times, probably for similar reasons too if you really dig into it. We laugh at there being three separate 'heads of St John the Baptist' in three different cathedrals, but they were deemed to be part of the 'hard to understand' Holy Trinity and therefore not to be discussed or questioned. The church authorities had a method to put an end to discussions about this sort of thing. They simply declared it a Holy mystery and would brook no further discussion on the topic. Chaucer writes about this in *The Pardoner's Tale*; in effect, the logic is 'it might be true, therefore let's go with it'. We also know that what was called pious theft was a thing and that some monasteries and cathedrals indulged in what were really quite dodgy practices to obtain relics and accoutrements of holy people. Fakery, fraud and just plain old making stuff up featured alongside arguably genuine relics of real people (genuine in the sense of being reliably a thing from a real person rather than an object with actual miraculous powers).

For my part, my own sense of hope – and I am in general an optimistic and cheery person – is very much tied up in my belief that technology is making and will continue to make the world a better place, and that if you look at the data, we're much better off than at any time in history, if taken in aggregate globally. If you were to tot up the pros and cons of the technological revolution in my lifetime, the net result would be positive, and quite considerably so. The world is getting better: it's more tolerant, more civilised and safer, even if the media, and our own cognitive biases, don't make it feel that way.

This is not to downplay or dismiss the many, many negatives of technological advance too, of course, or the terrible things that are clearly happening in many parts of the world, let alone the issues around climate change. We need to be comfortable not having a phone at hand: increasingly it seems that we're dependent on this expensive and demanding little communication box even to be human. We are, according to some, already cyborgs, unable to properly function without technology. (At least most of us are, I try to know the old ways of doing things as well as the new.) But at heart it's worth remembering that technology is a tool. It is not in itself positive or negative, good or evil: only the ways in which it's used can be described that way (at least, of course, until the Singularity and/or Skynet gains sentience, the machines turn on us, and all bets are off. Perhaps at that time the demand for old school medieval knights, as analogue as they come, will suddenly surge. You can't hack twelve feet of honest ash with a steel tip travelling at thirty miles an hour from the back of a speeding horse, though it might be a forlorn hope against titanium clad attack droids, it'd still look magnificent for a few moments).

Cars are an interesting example of technological progress. I'm not especially into cars, but it's really striking how few bad cars there are manufactured now as opposed to even thirty or forty years ago. In fact, I think that a mixture of competition and stringent safety standards means that anything less than a mediocre car simply wouldn't be sold as new, certainly not in first world markets. In contrast, when I started driving in the '80s there were all kinds of rustbuckets and death traps on the roads. I passed my driving test aged seventeen and was given my granny's Austin 1100, which I drove until the engine fell out. Literally fell out. I was holding the big spindly old-style steering wheel and I remember thinking, 'What was that noise?' and looking in the rear-view mirror, seeing a load of nuts and bolts, washers and fragments. I took my foot off the accelerator and then there was an enormous crash and the car went over itself somehow and landed with the back wheels on part of the engine. I had to walk to a nearby house (no mobile phones remember) and only the third one I tried would make a phone call for me to ask for help. They wouldn't let me in though. Chris's first car was our mum's cast-off yellow Mini Metro, which he similarly drove until the engine was coming off its support, and there was more Iron III Oxide than actual steel in the frame. Fast forward a few years and we shared a series of original two-seater Mazda MX-5s: great fun in the winter with the top down, dressed in twenty-seven layers, but you compare them to today's MX-5 and it's night and day. I used to leave mine unlocked in the futile hope that someone would try the doors to get in before slashing the fabric roof again. There was nothing to take, not even a radio, but the replacement soft top was costly. I suppose thieves are not very logical in their thought processes.

Cars also demonstrate that there's always a time when the new tech, counter-intuitively, lags behind the old tech. When the musket was invented, it was between five and ten times *less* effective than a longbow. Shorter range, less accurate, slower rate of shooting, probably more expensive to make, but could be used by anybody with an afternoon's training. The same can be seen with electric cars, which still need a lot of investment, R&D and infrastructure to be fully viable alternatives to combustion engine vehicles. They will get there, no doubt, but it will take a few years, and we'll look back on diesel and gasoline vehicles with astonishment, like we do smoking in pubs and restaurants today. I think the place will be a lot quieter and less smelly than ever before. Next we'll have to get rid of those toxic 'air fresheners' that some people seem to like. The ones that squirt out noxious 'fragrances' at regular intervals and poison us all, and the unbelievably polluting and noisy light leisure aircraft that plague us all in the summer months.

The pace of technological change in the video games industry is unrelenting, and 'next-gen' always seems to be a moving target. One day we'll learn not to call it next generation; each iteration of the various gaming consoles has been labelled next generation and that gets confusing when you've lived through them all (don't get me started on the naming of the Microsoft Xbox systems): no sooner have we arrived at the point we thought was the future than we see that there's an entirely new future on the distant horizon. Which is literally what a horizon it, it's the furthest we can see from where we are, rather than an actual place. We've been around long enough that the various gaming platforms transmogrify and they reinvent themselves quite regularly, so we're used to it, that things change is in itself unchanging. We have our own game engine technology which we can constantly update, so change of platform doesn't scare us in the slightest. We don't have to wait for anybody else's technology to catch up. We're lucky in some ways, I guess. It's ours, so we can work with whatever vendor comes along. There might be a big Chinese console one day, who knows? Our confidence comes from being flexible, which is one of the most important things in any business, not just ours.

Virtual reality is very exciting. It's an interesting frontier for media in general, not just games. It hasn't become mainstream yet in the way that we would hope. But it's still very early days. We're continuing to be involved with VR but we're not focussing entirely on it. VR is exciting but it has many challenges. Just as when film-making was starting out and there were many rules to learn and discover, or when radio first began, when the first books were published: when any new medium comes along it brings lots of unknowns, a lot of uncertainty and a whole new frontier to explore. That's the challenge VR has at the moment.

It's not perfect yet, but there are moments in this modern generation of VR headsets when you really feel you're *there* properly and immersively and completely. It's a very compelling technology when you're properly encompassed by a synthetic digital landscape. Each medium brings its own opportunities and challenges though, and VR is one of those where you can truly feel that you are exploring a different landscape, you have stepped through and into the system. I think VR will supplement existing mediums, rather than replace them, just like what happened when photography was invented. Paintings pre-photography were mostly illustrative: a king wanting a painting for posterity, a duke commissioning a portrait to hang on the wall, that kind of thing. Then photography came along, and it was much cheaper and easier to take a photo than it was to commission a painting. It didn't stop painting, though: just allowed it to expand into expressionism and all the other -isms in art. Painting as a medium was freed from the shackles of needing to represent something. All these new forms of painting sprang up at roughly the time when painting was freed up from having to paint a portrait of a rich merchant to buy your bread as an artist. Just as when the television was invented, there was and still is space for radio. One thing won't fully replace the other; it'll act as an additive. Some forms of storytelling have dwindled of course, but rarely have they disappeared entirely. VR can do something different.

VR could have transformative impacts on other industries too, such as tourism. Maybe people don't want to spend twelve hours flying to visit Angkor Wat. Maybe they want to visit Angkor Wat now, at lunchtime, wander around it for a couple of hours then come back to the real world, have a cappuccino and get on with their day. Imagine if you could visit Stonehenge without thousands of other tourists getting in your way: go back in history, get rid of that bloody road. Imagine seeing Rome at the height of Caligula. Imagine seeing the Medieval Popes. Imagine going any place you can think of and doing it safely and at your convenience.

A lot of people are still investing heavily in it, which is really exciting. In some ways, arguably, you could say that because the take up hasn't been ballistically fast, that's actually good for the longevity of it. With any new technology there's usually a very long period in which it's adopted. When colour TV was introduced, a lot of people didn't bother upgrading to a colour TV for many years. When asked why, they didn't see the point. The old black and white unit served them very well, and TV didn't dominate their lives that much. Therefore, I think it takes a while for many people to get used to any new idea. Some people are early adopters, and will wait patiently at midnight for a public relations-driven grand opening for some new device. Other people just can't be bothered. I used an old Nokia phone that was pretty much indestructible for much longer than my peer group thought sensible. The great thing about the games industry is it is no longer niche by any sensible definition of that word. We are one of the biggest creative industries in the world, so we can afford to sub-divide ourselves down a little bit. Like different categories of music, there are different categories of games and there should therefore be different categories of display. VR is one of those.

VR is always a challenge anyway, because it's a new landscape for games making and every VR game we do, or do with our colleagues, is a learning experience for pretty much everybody. There are things we think we know about games which, when you put them in VR, just don't work. There are things which you think aren't going to work, and then do in VR. The other challenge with VR is it's such a personal experience, and you really need to experience it with a headset on. It's always difficult to watch people playing a VR game and judge if they're having fun or not, because it doesn't really work the same way when you're watching the flat screen version of a VR game. When you have to wait for them to stop playing the game, take the helmet off, and tell you if it's good or not, it's a bit weird. You really need to go into VR to experience it. We've had some fantastic sights in the QA (quality assurance) booths where people are playing sessions, multiplayer sessions, whatever it might be. You'll have sixteen people with headsets on all somehow communicating with each other in this virtual world. But also all their brains look like they're partially downloaded into the game space. So you've got them all in the real world looking like aliens in odd helmets with these blue lights flickering everywhere, to my eyes resembling some sort of deep sea angler fish party under the sea, only without the frigid and dark water, but the players are experiencing something totally different. It is very much like something out of a sci-fi movie. It really is. It's real sci-fi, only it's not fiction. I'm not sure there's the right word for it. Science reality sounds a bit boring in comparison. It's wonderful to think we're at that stage of a new industry where in fifty years' time people will be looking at footage we've captured now and talking about this being a frontier of VR. Who knows if we'll even have headsets in another few years?

For older people, the pace of change even on levels way below VR can be relentless. I know of those who can't understand why Netflix doesn't have a *Radio Times*-style broadcast schedule, who can't work out e-mail as they don't think they're in the same place where the e-mail goes, and who don't like laptops as they get too hot when the machine is on top of their laps. It's easy to laugh at this, but it's not kind, and this type of bewilderment at change has been a constant factor throughout history. I'm aware how lucky I am not just to love computers anyway, but also to be part of the generation which has spanned the analogue–digital divide. We're the only ones who went through it all – early PCs, punch tape computers, Walkmans, DVDs, Blu-Ray, mobile phones, smartphones – and that's rather a privilege to have had a ringside seat at this technological explosion. I still don't understand the attraction of certain types of social media though. I'm not sure there is any value in some of it outside it being a shared experience.

Change is hard for many people, and the easiest way to deal with it is denial. Just don't acknowledge it at all and it'll go away (it won't). Our brains have evolved the wetware that is fundamentally designed to keep us alive and not be eaten by lions: they're not necessarily wired up for the modern corporate world. Our brains have lots of shortcuts that work well enough to keep some of us alive and out of the stomach of hyenas. Evolution as a process is not about achieving perfection, or even being very good, it's about being OK enough to survive and reproduce; sometimes barely OK is sufficient. We have big brains, but in terms of total biomass on the planet beetles are substantially better at being beetles than we are at being humans. Evolution doesn't make us perfect: along with the hand of random chance (nothing can evolve to survive a tree falling on it suddenly), the process simply sorts out failures from successes and lets them breed again and repeat the selection process. We're good enough survival machines, albeit with very limited senses. We only see a tiny bit of the electromagnetic spectrum: we can't see infrared (which means we could see in the dark as some animals can) or ultraviolet (so we can't see the sun on foggy days as some animals can). Our sense of smell is absurdly inferior to that of dogs, whose smellscape shifts and blurs depending on which way the wind is blowing and who can 'see' past events in smell trails, or if someone is well or ill from their odour. Their whole world has a time dimension as they can sense a scene's age too: they overlay curtains of scent. They can also detect human fear and stress from the smells we give off. They are much more dimensionally capable than we are. We can just about perceive four dimensions, but not beyond that. We can't hold our breath underwater for much longer than a few dozens of seconds unless we train for it, then we might manage a few minutes; we can't eat rancid meat without getting ill as our stomachs are not acidic enough like a dog's is. Mostly we can't even live outside in many climates found on the planet without artificial shelter. Humans are very good at doing certain things though; we just need to be careful not to judge other creatures by our human standards.

Dolphins, to take just one example, are aware of much more than we are. They can see inside people due to the ability of their echolocation system to pick up the shape and state of our internal organs. It's not strictly 'seeing', of course, as much as 'detecting', but still: a dolphin can detect the beat of your heart and the passage of your blood through your blood vessels. I would love to have echolocation. If we had echolocation we probably wouldn't have discovered fire, as it would have bypassed our inability to see in the dark. 2000 AD had a story called 'Visible Man', in which someone's skin became transparent: but this would not be in any way extraordinary to a dolphin. The medical profession might have developed much earlier though, and what we might see as beauty would literally be more than skin deep.

If you plot the ratio of body size to male testicle size among mammals, those species with the largest sized testicles relative to their body size all have harem structures (such as one stallion to between about four and seven mares) – all apart from us humans; that is, in most cultures. Our body size/testicle ratio should put us in the big harem section, but instead we typically have a pair of adults to look after children, and breeding successfully, passing your genes on to the next generation, is the golden rule of the process of evolution. No matter how fast, or clever, or strong or far-seeing you might be, if you can't or don't pass on those characteristics to the next generation, you might as well be dead as far as the process of evolution is concerned. (This is an oversimplification actually as social behaviour from genetically linked non-breeders can benefit the success of the 'breeders' which in turn can benefit the genes you and they carry – social insects come to mind, along with naked mole rats, and many academic books have been written on this phenomenon.) Pair bonding is an evolutionary strategy for slow-developing big-brained humans. Horses can stand in a few hours, and run in a day or so after being born. Human children are, in terms of self-care, so useless for so long (some might jokingly suggest for about eighteen years or more).

I don't just love horses: I'm also fascinated by them. How would our society have evolved if we were horses, needing to eat high volume, low nutrient fodder for eight hours a day? (I'm aware that there are parts of the world where this seems to have come to pass for humans too, but that's certainly not a need.) Humans are the only species which definitively has sex just for pleasure; a few others might. Our society revolves around food and sex, but the entire structure of our society might be very different if both those are seen as purely functional, or if women were just violently and aggressively not interested in sex or emotional entanglement with men at all for most of their oestrus cycle as are mares. Somebody should write a science fiction book about that society.

Humans don't radically change over time in many ways: they're mostly the same from generation to generation. In medieval times, for example, they knew the symptoms of diabetes: they'd taste urine for the 'honey disease', as diabetes made urine taste sweet, or they put urine out to see if the ants were attracted to it. The job of urine taster was one that existed in many places. Conversely some things do change in unusual ways. To take several examples pretty much at random: salmon and brown wholemeal bread were peasant food in the Middle Ages, cooked on charcoal rather than an open fire. Now they're the most middle-class things imaginable and totally Waitrose. Medieval moats weren't just water, nice fish and lily pads: they were filled with all kinds of garbage and infection risk, such as animal entrails, the contents of some long drop castle latrines and dead things. Attacking across a moat would have been pretty horrible. You might have thought human waste would be a major part of that too, and it was but human waste was also vital for the manufacture of saltpetre, which in turn was vital for the manufacture of gunpowder. Human faeces were known as night soil, and the gong farmers who collected them had exclusive legal rights to your faeces from the moment it left your body. Poop and pee were often collected separately and were industrial resources, so not lightly wasted. Piss, as it was often called, without it being a crude term, was also collected and sold as a modest source of revenue. Hence the phrase, 'So poor they don't even have a pot to piss in'.

We have also lost the communal rhythms of work, not just weekly with market days but also seasonally, where many workers (not just farm workers but builders and some other manual labourers too) were sacked in the autumn and had to eke out a living over the winter until being hired again in the spring. Some summer and winter occupations were intertwined too; for example tile makers in the summer became hedge repairers in the winter.

Maritime technology has arguably progressed much more slowly than other forms of transport. A medieval peasant wouldn't recognise a car or a plane probably (although a horseless carriage and a big metal bird might be explainable after a few moments), but he would recognise even the most advanced ship as being from the same mould as any boat he was used to seeing, just a lot bigger and made with what he would probably be most astonished by, the vast fortune of steel that it's made from.

You can see the same thing on a much smaller timescale these days. A significant proportion of young adults I work with these days can't drive and never bother to learn: why would they, when they can be reliant on taxis, Uber and public transport? So the same person at work can end up being the designated driver again and again as no one else knows how. Getting a car for me and my generation and social group was a rite of passage. When there were only wire connected phones called landlines, and those would be answered by your parents probably, you'd agree to meet someone at a given time and place, and you had to be there, so being able to get there on time was vital, which as often as not meant driving. Driving to places has been substituted by social media and easy access to communications.

Take cash, too, which is looking more and more like an anachronism. A cashless society has several benefits for a government: it makes it harder for people to avoid tax, and it also saves a (relatively small) amount because making physical money costs, well money. It gets worn out and needs to be replaced. Throughout much of later human history, money as physical cash has more or less kept pace with technology, in terms of the ability to provide a means of exchange which is both relatively easy to manufacture and relatively hard to counterfeit. Increasingly, however, money has become digital – plenty of shops already refuse to take cash (which I think is technically still illegal here in the UK) – and will only become more so with the rise not just of digital money but digital currencies too. The likes of Bitcoin and all the other digital currencies are even more removed from actual reality in some ways. They are for the moment perhaps more comprehensible as very volatile and risky investments than as a currency, but that does not mean that this will be the case forever.

In terms of change, and at the time of writing, Brexit has been pushed out of the headlines in the last year or two by Covid, but of course it has presented, and continues to present, certain challenges to our sector, as it does to most industries. I'm always concerned about how best to manage big and rapid changes, but the most challenging situation in any state of transition is when you don't really know what those changes are going to be and therefore have to expect the worst. It's a bit like driving into dense fog. You have to go slowly and be careful, and your sense of perspective and direction can get woefully muddled because you can't see very far ahead at all. To start with, post-referendum, we had a few of our non-UK-born members of staff reasonably concerned about their jobs and future, but that seems to have settled down a bit now. If anything, we noticed a bit of upturn in people applying to work for us. That's slightly disguised by the fact that we're quite well known and we make some high profile titles, so I'm not sure we are a bellwether for general attitudes in that area. Subsequently the rise in hybrid working from home and the office seems to be settling down, and new ways of communicating have rapidly established themselves. Before this pandemic, I'm not sure I'd had more than a handful of video meetings; now they seem natural and much easier than actually travelling to meet someone in what used to be called real life.

The EU is an interesting issue to wrestle with. On one level I can see the huge benefits a big trading block can bring with its collective bargaining powers; on the other hand you've got places like Catalonia wanting to do their own thing and gain independence. There seems to be pressure from some groups to split into units smaller than the present national geographic boundaries, many of which were formed around the treaty table post one of the many wars that have regularly plunged parts of this end of the continent into chaos. Especially into units where people have a shared cultural history in a unique way. Historically of course Europe was much more subdivided than it is today. Places like the fascinating and tragic Languedoc region of what is now southern France had its own religion, culture and language, and was destroyed by an actual crusade against the Cathars of the region. I'm slightly surprised that this region of France doesn't have a significant separatist movement. It may do, but it's not one that I've heard about. One of the things medieval history has taught me is how much change Europe has gone through over time, how borders have been drawn and redrawn and cultures wiped out or buried, but also how much it has endured and how flexible it has been in dealing with these changes.

Europe is not the EU, though the two terms are often used interchangeably. It's a brute fact that we're part of Europe; we're a very big offshore island but we are part of the geography of Europe. We're not digging an even bigger ditch and sailing offshore, we're still going to be there. We are still going to be trading with people: it's just what type and scale of trade barriers will be put into place by politicians that will impact us all. And in any times of change there are always business opportunities if you know where to look, and because computer games are exciting and creative and interesting there will always be these opportunities. The world's a big place. Europe and North America as markets for us are fairly stable. They're big, they're important, and they're mature, but they're stable, and it's hard to grow your market share in saturated environments like that. The markets that we expect to grow and change are Brazil, India, Russia, Latin America, China, hopefully the vastness that is Africa one day soon: these all have great potential where big change can happen rapidly. The good thing is we export our creative work world-wide. We're a massive net exporter. So I guess you could argue we are good for UK PLC because only about ten percent of our sales are in the UK, which means ninety percent comes from outside our island fortress and brings in cash from outside.

One of my major concerns that I have for our progress as a species is the collapse of nuance and the rise of extremism of thought in all its forms, religious, political and knowledge denial. I think the decrease in enlightenment values about logic and reason and discourse means a lot of people seem to become very tribal very quickly. Just looking at the polarisation in politics for example, frankly neither 'wing' has got the answers exclusively. They've all got problems. As usual, in life, reality is more of a middle ground position. Social media and the systems that drive engagement at the expense of quality or value are a big part of the disconnect and divide. If social media disappeared tomorrow, how long would it take for us to readjust? Probably a matter of days, certainly for those who knew a pre-internet age. Younger people would find it more difficult, just as they tend to text rather than call, but they'd adjust too. I removed several types of social media from my phone because I found it far too intrusive and demanding on my time, ultimately a bit limiting and a hideously unproductive time sink. I do still use social media, mostly Facebook and Twitter and the community on my YouTube channel, but I am draconian in removing content that I dislike. It's my diary after all, and freedom of speech has bugger all to do with it. I'd tell nutters to leave my property if they misbehaved in the real world too. Nowadays a phone call seems urgent, even rude for some, forcing the other person to answer. A text message allows the recipient to read and reply at their own convenience, but even punctuation can be misinterpreted. Apparently there are some social circles where the full stop at the end of a text is considered aggressive for some reason that escapes me. (Not an aggressive full stop by the way.)

The important thing to realise about progress and hope is that you have to look back as well as forward to get a true perspective of your travel. I'm not beholden to new tech just for the sake of it. My favourite gadget of all is my penknife, the design of which probably goes back well beyond Ancient Rome. I carry a small, folding knife whenever I am allowed to. I use it dozens of times a day: for cutting twine off bales of hay, opening letters, digging dirt out of bolt holes, chopping apples, and cutting up pies to eat. It's a low tech gadget, but incredibly useful. It gets sharpened every few days. There's nothing more dangerous than a blunt knife, especially a folding one, and under current laws, it's not sensible for it to be a locking one which would be a lot safer in use.

The first time I encountered a real computer was one donated by big business to my school in the late 1970s, and it took up a whole converted classroom. That room was open only to those who were members of the computer club, which meant I could also be inside at break in filthy weather (and if you were a member you got a special laminated membership card too). I was hugely interested in the output as well as the machinery itself. Fast forward a few more years and you could only buy a few different types of personal computer. Amongst others there were the Sinclair Spectrum, the Commodore 64, and I managed to persuade my parents to invest in an Atari 800. When the weather was bad I would stay inside, making model soldiers and model landscapes and play early computer games. Fast forward even more years and to set up our business we bought a £3,000 computer. You could choose 40Mb or the 'more than you will ever need' 80Mb hard drive. We went for the bigger one to make it future proof, which it wasn't. Like desk space or shelves, you will never have enough. Think what you could never possibly use and then double it. That still won't be right.

But now... Well, in one respect *Nineteen Eighty-Four* didn't go far enough: Orwell never imagined that we would pay for the privilege of carrying our own surveillance measures around with us. I've mentioned yachting holidays out loud in conversation and then adverts for them have started showing up in my news feed. Just a mention in conversation, no Google search or anything. I'm pretty sure they're listening when they're not supposed to be. Maybe I'm wrong and I'm just seeing things where they aren't. Cognitive biases exist and we're very good pattern-recognition machines as I've mentioned before. However, I think they are listening if they can. Ethics and big business seem to be distant bedfellows for some. Mobile phones are radios, after all. When Edward Snowden revealed the extent of US government surveillance, one of the programmes he spoke about was called Boundless Informant! It was almost too perfect, like something out of Le Carre or Ludlum.

Progress always seems scarcely imaginable when looking into the future, hard to comprehend when going through it, and inevitable with hindsight. We're fond of saying things like 'what did we do before e-mail?', but of course we managed perfectly well. In decades to come people will say 'what did we do before neural implants?' On a similar note, our attitudes concerning the past are often that it was either a hallowed golden age or an exotic time full of ritual and mysticism. But of course since so much of our lives are mundane, it follows that the same would be true of any period. When the Mayan script was finally deciphered, it revealed that a Peruvian cup ringed with symbols and drawings which had been considered a priceless religious relic actually read something like 'this is my hot chocolate drinking mug' plus the owner's name. It was basically a decorated novelty mug. The same mundane, human and also thoroughly wonderful messages from the past have been found with Viking axes and the runes engraved in them, which have turned out to mean, 'This is Olaf's axe and these runes were carved by his friend Jonas'. There's even some graffiti carved by a no doubt bored Varangian guard at the great Hagia Sophia complex that just says, 'Olaf was 'ere'.

My horses are my escapes both from stress and pressure of work and also back into the past. I've jousted at the Tower of London at the exact same spot where Henry VIII did, wearing museum-quality reproduction steel armour, sweating and nervous – in other words, feeling more or less exactly the same feelings he would have and experiencing what he'd have experienced, though he was an absolute monarch so maybe his thoughts were very different than mine, or maybe not; even monarchs are humans. I used to drive down the Fosse Way from Leicestershire to Oxford and my studies at St John's College, six times a year at the beginning and end of each term. Every time I did I'd ponder the past and think, 'This is a Roman road where 2,000 years ago Roman soldiers would have been marching along, minds wandering probably. I wonder if they ever wondered what would happen in 2,000 years' time,' and 2,000 years from now someone will be in a flying car wondering what happened here two millennia before, and that would be a forgotten me thinking about an unnamed Roman legionary. It's a universal theme: always has been and always will be. You could stack plans of the world on top of each other and trace where people were in their own time: find yourself standing in a place where a Celtic warrior once fought, or living on a farm which was once deep inside a glacier. Any physical space is only available for temporary occupation: there have been others passing this way before and there will be others here afterwards. It amuses me, fascinates me, and makes me slightly sad that any of us only get to see a tiny fraction of a tiny bit of existence.

Chapter Twelve

Valour

VALOUR COVERS MANY things in addition to physical bravery. In business, for example, the need to be brave is obvious: you need to have the ability to charge forward, seize the opportunity and do the best that you can with it, as well as exploring new territories and seeking out new markets. Moving forwards, making decisions knowing they may be wrong is an essential component of being a leader, but over the course of the previous eleven chapters we have discussed most of these one way or another, so for this final chapter I shall concentrate on 'valour' in the most obvious sense of physical bravery: and nowhere is this more obvious than in jousting.

Jousting was the original extreme sport. I imagine people from all walks of life enjoyed watching the wealthy beat each other up on horseback. Some have said that jousting was more popular than football back in its heyday. I've tried to explain the sport as a bit like playing golf on a skateboard whilst wearing very heavy clothes, and having someone else trying to hit you at the same time. It's hard to explain, and probably even harder to do right. Jousting's one of the few extreme fighting sports where there's no defence. You just need to look after what you can do, and if somebody's going to hit you they're going to hit you, hard, sometimes very hard indeed. Business is like that: you can't account for whatever other people are going to do, so you just have to expect that things will happen and be prepared to roll with the hits, or in the case of actual jousting, withstand them and not fall off.

My realisation that proper modern jousting existed dates from going to see a historical event at Kelmarsh Hall, meeting some jousting knights from a group called Destrier, arranging to see them practise and thinking I'd like to do that. The rest is history (quite literally). Destrier competed with what are called breaking lances with replaceable ends, mostly for budgetary reasons, but also for safety. A few years later a handful of us decided to try to joust with real solid wooden lances complete with metal tips, just to see if it could be done and survived. I volunteered to be the first person in modern times to be hit by one of these real lances in a practice session at my farm in Northamptonshire. In so doing and in competing with a colleague at several castles later that same year I became one of the first two people in about 400 years to do it properly, jousting with a solid wooden lance with a heavy metal end called a coronel, in real competition in public, unscripted, real physical combat. It was thrilling, stressful, physically demanding and on reflection potentially lethal. Back in the day senior church figures suggested that those that died in tournament, as opposed to whilst on crusade, should not be buried in hallowed ground. This was widely ignored and quietly dropped as a rule. Rich powerful fathers were unlikely to avoid burying their sons properly if they died in sporting combat after all.

Some people think jousting is rather like pro wrestling, all for show and with no real danger. It's not, but it also is a little. Pro wrestling is a hugely physical activity with genuine pain and danger, though not as much as you might expect from the over-acted faces of the wrestlers themselves, and whilst there is co-ordination between the fighters, there's also a lot of improvisation and performance presentation going on. Jousting shares the pomp and presentation, but the actual passes, the runs, the gallops down the tilt rail are unplanned. (Some theatrical jousting done at theme park type places is scripted, though the consequences of physics still create a level of danger.) The jousting I do is unscripted and full contact. We really are striking at each other at speed on horseback with long sticks. Showmanship is and was also a big part of jousting tournaments. Costumes were made for the knight's entire entourage, his tent was lined with solid gold and needed sixteen men to lift it, and so on. Some of this kind of stuff lives on in the Palio horse race in Siena, where the procession before the race is as much of a spectacle as the race itself. In business also presentation matters. Great content badly presented is not as well received as that same great content well presented.

Jousting injuries are on the rise as the sport's popularity grows: *Game of Thrones* has a lot to do with both of these. The danger comes because people see it and aren't properly prepared to do it, with the wrong kit, the wrong training and often the wrong attitude too. You wouldn't go skydiving without having expert tuition and a training course or two under your belt; nor should you bestride a destrier and slam into another person at a combined speed of fifty miles an hour, without being thoroughly trained and properly equipped. I take my preparations very seriously. Even so, Rebellion has a 'key man' insurance policy in place for me in case the worst happens. There have even been some deaths in jousting, both historically and more recently, but again these have usually come through a combination of inexperience, the wrong safety equipment, and a lot of bad luck. Historically the fatal shot was usually from the lance fragments going through the eye slot of the helmet, as happened to Henri II of France, but if someone doesn't know what they're doing then even a fall from a horse can be fatal. I've seen people joust in very little armour, but that is just crazy to me. Having the throat poorly protected is asking for trouble, as is using a helmet designed for foot combat.

At a tournament I usually find myself arming up in front of an audience, which is an issue as what I'm putting on is in reality medieval safety equipment, and ideally you don't want too many distractions. People ask if I have a specific arming or tournament preparation routine: no, not really, not that I can think of, though the armour does go on in a specific order. I get asked the same questions by the public all the time, such as, 'Is it hot?', 'Does it hurt?', 'Is it hard?' and, 'Do you enjoy it?'. The answers are yes, yes, yes and yes. One cheeky small boy asked me what would happen if my arm got chopped off. I said I'd hope to go immediately to hospital, but might probably die. He followed that up with, 'What would happen if your leg got chopped off?'

I have usually jousted on either my ex-polo pony called Segunda, or on my YouTube famous horsey companion Warlord. Since I've been riding a long time, if I have to ride a new horse then that's not too much of an issue, though you always err on the side of caution to begin with. It's better to under ride a new horse than over ride it. The main issue is a difference in the launch acceleration of each horse and the final top speed. Both Warlord and Segunda have gone very fast at times, but others go much more slowly, and that changes the timing of my lance lowering. Sometimes it takes a couple of runs to get my eye in, sometimes you can get under an opponent's lance if you go fast enough and they're not expecting it. Obviously the faster you hit the bigger the impact too.

I like jousting events, especially the ones I do that are, as I said, unscripted and authentic. English Heritage do good ones, usually. There are entertaining 'medieval style pageant jousts' with a white knight and a black knight that are fun theatre, but they owe more to Hollywood of old than history of old; they're in effect re-enactments of classic movie tropes. The horses are real and well trained though and the riders are highly skilled, they're just not performing with historical intent.

Technically, to have your own heraldry requires that you either inherit it from your father or have it granted by an actual herald. Anybody using real heraldry at an event that is not their own and has not been properly granted is actually breaking the law and liable to punishment, though I'm pretty sure the powers that be have better things to do that arrest a reenactor for pretending to be a knight by bearing arms. There was a time in history though where that might have been a very serious crime indeed. My real heraldry is designed and granted to me by a herald whose official title is Bluemantle Pursuivant and is a member of the College of Arms. It consists of a unicorn horn to represent my love of horses and mythology, and two lances, on a broad red vertical stripe. I wear a steel replica of an original medieval suit of armour that was made to measure for me, and usually have jousted a dozen or so weekends every year. The lance, made of wood but with a steel tip, is about twelve feet long, and when you're both riding a stallion fast at each other, that's a closing speed of around forty to possibly fifty miles an hour. Imagine leaning out of a car window holding a pole and hitting a wall with it. The impact would be the same. If the other person's lance hits you at that speed, it hurts. I've never been struck from the saddle (yet that is), but I have taken three people to the ground over the years, and never even once hit a horse.

In practice, I can reliably strike a four-inch target pretty much all the time, and some of the time, maybe one in ten attempts, stick a sharp lance through the narrow eye-slit on a medieval helmet, on horseback, travelling at speed. That eye slit is about the thickness of half a finger, or perhaps a third of an inch, maybe half? I practise using melons mounted on spikes, and set myself the task of nailing a four-inch target on a swivel: not just once but again and again. I'd hope that the original knights were at least as good as me, but like everything it probably varied from person to person, based on their aptitude, base skill and the amount they practised.

My first suit of costume mail was made for me by my grandmother, hello gran, when I was a boy. It was home made string maille, made by knitting a loose wool costume, and then sprayed with silver paint. It's actually how professional string maille is made even today, little did we know. I loved it. Now I have steel suits of armour custom made for me. They are significantly more expensive than a very expensive Savile Row suit. A high quality harness ('suit of armour' is a Victorian term) designed to keep you alive in the joust would cost a bare minimum of £10,000, but more realistically, if it's a fancy one perhaps £25,000 to £30,000. You're talking about a lot of money for armour that doesn't really have much use except stopping you from dying when you joust (which on reflection is probably money well spent). So not that versatile, but what it does do is pretty important. Of course, it's going to get damaged and needs to be repaired too. The armour I joust in is late 15th-century Milanese armour, based on a version of what is known as the Avaunt harness. In total I have four full harnesses so far of various periods. I also have plenty of maille, helmets and swords, again of different historical periods from the most basic Norman conquest maille hauberk and nasal helm, to the later full steel mesh 'onesie' that predates the plate enhancements that came in later. There's a general rule that once you get into this area of enthusiasm, it's not possible to have too much kit. I've spent far too much money over the years on my armour and kit and horses, and arguably a small part of the complex business motivation for deciding to acquire and work a farm was the land for adventures.

My targe (shield) is probably too small, historically speaking, and in need a lot of repairs. It also needs to be painted better but it does seem to get very bashed each season. If I was using solid lances (the end part of some types of lance is designed to shatter) I'd need to have a thicker one. When it comes to helmets I prefer an armet with a solid, unhinged wrapper that protects my face and throat. The design of mine is largely based on the 'Battle of San Romano' painting by the Florentine artist Paolo Uccello. It can't open up no matter what impact happens as it's just a shaped sheet of steel, but it is heavy and very restrictive. Helmets reduce your sight quite dramatically, for obvious reasons, and also how you can move your head and neck, as well as restricting your upper body movement too. You do get used to it, but sometimes, especially on a hot day at the end of a long weekend of jousting, it can get troubling and claustrophobic as well as hot and sweaty, and literally stinking. Knights of old clearly looked magnificent, but they almost certainly ponged to high heaven after combat (having said that, being a bit smelly was probably not high on their lists of concerns during real battle). Some people say that the movement of the horse as you approach the tilt actually slightly increases your field of vision, but I've never noticed that myself. My focus narrows down to the target I'm trying to hit with the lance tip and making the two meet: I never notice the other combatant's lance at all until it hits me, and even then the impact might just be me hitting them.

To have armour made to a museum quality and wear it on a horse in the heat in simulated battle: there's nothing else like it. One of the interesting things about real armour, which you don't know until you wear it, is how claustrophobic it can get in some circumstances. The 15th-century illustrated manuscript *How a Man Shall Be Armed* recommends that a knight 'take his ease' before suiting up: calls of nature were definitely more easily taken out of armour than in it, though it is possible to go to the toilet in full harness if you have to. It's just quite noisy. I'd also recommend using the disabled portaloo toilet too as the extra room inside makes everything easier. Leaving a temporary toilet at an event in armour also provides a funny photograph for visitors, which may or may not amuse you depending on your perspective on this sort of thing. Once, when re-enacting the mythical contest between Saint George and the dragon, my saddle broke in two. The saddle tree snapped and that meant that it was pushing down through the padding into Warlord's back. I had no way of knowing how injured he might be getting so, as he bolted in panic, I hurled myself off him as soon as I could. Trying to land safely whilst also getting as far away from him as possible otherwise I might have risked injuring him if I fell. With six stone of armour on me (about half my body weight), I sounded like a shelf of tin plates crashing to the floor, which, frankly, was precisely what it was. I was moderately badly hurt, with two cracked ribs, and some nastily pulled muscles, but after checking Warlord was OK now the pressure of my weight was off him, I trudged back into the arena and slew the dragon to the amusement of the crowd. Apparently the dragon had danced the Macarena twice and was quickly becoming the crowd favourite.

Someone on the internet suggested that armour must have been counterproductive, because a nimble unarmoured swordsman would move quicker. But that ignores the fact that someone in armour is basically a medieval tank and would rarely fight alone. If you were unarmoured you could swing at me with a sword, but you couldn't penetrate the armour and would do almost nothing to me unless you were very lucky or skilful with the point and aimed for a gap. Meanwhile, I'd stick you once or twice, then you're bleeding, then I'd take off your hand with my axe and it's over. Even being punched by a plate gauntlet might be enough to take an unarmoured combatant down, and some gauntlets had spiked gadlings or knuckles, presumably for exactly that reason. In the UK these days knuckle dusters are illegal; in medieval times, knights had them built into their gauntlets.

As I said in the previous chapter, when I'm jousting in fantastic places like the Tower of London or Kenilworth Castle, it's time travel. I'm a re-enactor, I'm not pretending to be from the past. I'm a modern person with modern sensibilities, who is riding in harness and wielding a lance but trying to recapture some of what it must have been like back then. This is what I try to show in my Modern History TV videos on YouTube and elsewhere: even the smallest sense of what it was really like. Theory and book learning are great, but there is something special about testing it out, about personally experiencing it and trying to articulate that to an audience who may not have the opportunity to do so for themselves. A lot of medieval historians have never wielded a lance, nor worn armour in real combat. You can, with a bit of imagination, guess how it might have been, but there is no substitute for personal testimony in my opinion, and that's highly subjective, but useful.

I reimagine the heavy cavalry charges, the archery assault, the shield walls, the mud and blood, the dysentery and terror. Even the best movies surely only get across a fraction of what it must have been like. Medieval battle appears to have often descended into medieval brawling. Knights sometimes killed each other's horses before eventually ending up rolling around on the ground trying to stab each other in the face with a specialised weapon. That weapon was the Rondel dagger, which has a long, narrow, often triangular cross section stabbing blade with a broad flat disk above and below the grip and looks like a wicked nail. Its sole purpose and design is to stab someone to death. (You could use it to carve something I suppose, or eat with it, but it'd do a lousy job at those.) They'd punch it into each other, seeking the fleshy bits left exposed by a joint in the armour, or wrench open an enemy's visor and plunge the dagger into their naked face. It was brutal, horrible, direct. Then there was the pollaxe, which was a spike, an axe blade and a hammer all in one and mounted on a roughly five or six-foot haft. You could poke, hook, stab and pound. It was very much a giant Swiss Army knife for bloodletting. Using a pollaxe on a dummy target head is like hitting a chocolate Easter egg with a hammer. Slightly shocking, terrifying and easy.

We have so much to learn about training both riders and horses for battle. Most of it was not written down, so what I do is conjectural, but given that horses haven't really changed much in a few hundred years, I assume back then they'd have similar challenges as we do today. Every aspect of this horse training basically involves doing small things in small increments, building up the horse's confidence until you get to your final training destination. I'm sure police horses are trained in ways that would be familiar to war horse trainers centuries ago. There are many ways to use a sword and lance from horseback and a few of those were actually written down in the medieval period. These fight books or combat manuals mostly concentrate on foot combat, but some of them have a little on-horse based fighting. Enough to get us started, but lacking in depth and detail.

Early centre-held circular shields on their own will rotate in the grip when hit, but will do so much less when linked with other shields, perhaps confirming these were for close formations of footmen and the effectiveness of a shield wall and demonstrating the value of numbers and mutual reinforcement. In my opinion the use of a shield also varies a lot depending on whether the holder is on foot or horseback. I believe one of the reasons for the development from round to 'kite-shaped' shield was to allow the rider to hold the reins with the same single arm also supporting and controlling the shield. A shield wall became stronger the more layers it had, and soldiers in such a wall would also use natural features such as woods, marshes and rivers to stop the ends being outflanked.

The Vikings used what was called a boar snout formation, which was effective at punching through a static shield wall. This was basically what it said on the tin, a wedge of closely packed men which concentrated immense pressure at the chap selected or volunteered to be at the point and who was pretty much just pushed through the enemy line at a given point in the enemy's defence. To be at the head of the boar snout would have likely been certain death, but would also have been prestigious and heroic. I've tried it on a very small scale while filming the YouTube videos, and even then I was lifted off my feet.

These are the kinds of things they leave out of history books. History is so fascinating, and yet it's often taught in such a dry way: lists of kings with the same name, these were the queens, these were the land reforms, this is the date (which is often an educated guess rather than being necessarily true). This isn't just a medieval gripe, either. Take the way the Battle of Trafalgar is taught. It's all about the tactics of the battle and Nelson's heroism, which is fine, but remember this too: some of the men in his fleet had been at sea for more or less three years and they were absolutely itching for a fight. It's not too much of a stretch to imagine them chanting, 'Come and have a go if you think you're hard enough' at Villeneuve's fleet, as though they were rival football fans well up for a ruck. These men were skilled sailors, sure, but they were also rough men who would fight anytime, anywhere and anyhow.

In any war you'll likely find three types of soldier: the ones who relish trying to kill the other side, the ones who go along with it but don't want the consequences of killing, and the ones who won't do it at all. The ratios are usually something like 5-90-5. There have been cases of people not firing a single shot even when involved in combat which lasted hours: some of the US soldiers found dead at Hamburger Hill in Vietnam still had full magazines, and some of those killed at Gettysburg had muskets full of bullets. Some of those could have been malfunctions, or panic preventing you from clicking your safety off perhaps, but, according to research, the vast majority of humans don't really want to fight and kill at all. How much more difficult is it then to hack or stab someone to death?

Perhaps there's even a strange kind of valour in that, too: a refusal to take another's life even when that refusal will almost certainly cost you your own. In some circumstances that would be very chivalrous.

Epilogue

THERE'S A WELL-KNOWN meme which helps to indicate how fast history moves. It involves subtracting the amount of years you've been alive from your birth year to show the events you are as close to chronologically in the past as you are to those today. I was born in 1964, which means that I am as close to 1907 as I am to today: in technological terms, a year most famous for being that in which Marconi first sent radio messages across the Atlantic from Ireland to Nova Scotia.

Marconi would doubtless be amazed to see what can be done with technology these days, but the pace of change is so much quicker than in his time that in another fifty-seven years' time all the things we regard as impossibly cutting edge will seem as anachronistic as the stuff of yesteryear does to us. It's unlikely (barring a great leap forward in anti-ageing and/or cryogenics) that I'll still be around to see that, but if we narrow the time frame a little down to the thirty years or so I've been involved in the video games business – well, I'd certainly hope to be around for another thirty years, and I can't see a situation in which I wouldn't be interested in what's going on in the industry and wouldn't be excited by all the avenues which games can go in.

If this book has left you with anything, I hope it's this: that it's almost impossible to be too interested in this world and all there is in it. I've approached the world at various times as a games maker, a zoologist, an artist, an historian, a modern medieval knight, and much more. Each approach and discipline has taught me different things and gifted me with knowledge. There is an almost infinite amount of variety in this world, and though I grew up reading fantasy novels and still enjoy helping create fictional universes, this wonderful world right here, right now, is a good one.

I'm an optimist, and I believe in humanity – in our passion, our reason, our intelligence and our determination. But at the same time I believe that any interest in the world has to be balanced by reasonable questioning of that world. (I don't mean signing up to any and all conspiracy theories: if you question something then you have to apply the same standards to any alternative narrative you choose to adhere to as well, and too many conspiracy theories are so obviously batshit that no sensible person could possibly believe in them.) No: I mean that you should always look for the path less trodden or the angle less examined. Rebellion for me has never been just a company, a slogan or a logo: it's a state of mind, and I hope that never stops.

Banners advance, a quest awaits!